It's Not About Age, It's About Attitude

A Simple Guide for Baby Boomers

Sue Asti Cortesi

BALBOA.
PRESS
A DIVISION OF HAY HOUSE

Balboa Press books may be ordered through booksellers or by contacting:

Balboa Press
A Division of Hay House
1663 Liberty Drive
Bloomington, IN 47403
www.balboapress.com
1 (877) 407-4847

Because of the dynamic nature of the Internet, any web addresses or links contained in this book may have changed since publication and may no longer be valid. The views expressed in this work are solely those of the author and do not necessarily reflect the views of the publisher, and the publisher hereby disclaims any responsibility for them.

The author of this book does not dispense medical advice or prescribe the use of any technique as a form of treatment for physical, emotional, or medical problems without the advice of a physician, either directly or indirectly. The intent of the author is only to offer information of a general nature to help you in your quest for emotional and spiritual well-being. In the event you use any of the information in this book for yourself, which is your constitutional right, the author and the publisher assume no responsibility for your actions.

Any people depicted in stock imagery provided by Thinkstock are models, and such images are being used for illustrative purposes only. Certain stock imagery © Thinkstock.

ISBN: 978-1-5043-3112-8 (sc)
ISBN: 978-1-5043-3113-5 (e)

Print information available on the last page.

Balboa Press rev. date: 04/29/2015

Dedication

Remembering Gwen Townley Speaks

1949-2007

She was a true sister of the soul, her physical presence is dearly missed but her spirit is ever present thank heavens. Gwennie your perseverance and your love will never be forgotten.

"The Universe is unfolding as it should." – Gwen Speaks

PREFACE

Your thoughts are your power!

As a life coach and a senior citizen myself I have been prompted to write this short and simple guide with great enthusiasm after working with clients and discussing with other seniors just what most people would like to achieve in the senior years ahead.

If we can change the face of aging to being an adventure just by tweaking our thoughts so we feel good continually it would be wonderful wouldn't it?

I have compiled several areas of life that have been the most consistent in my work with clients and how they would like to make their lives the most positive they can.

This guide is written for all who would like to bring ease to the mind body and spirit by seeing life and aging as the adventure it can be.

INTRODUCTION

It is funny about the perceptions handed down every generation about aging isn't it? There have always been definite ideas taught about what happens when we age, what to expect and how to act.

Who says these are hard and fast rules which must be followed?

What if we change our attitude in areas of our lives that will make a difference in the way we age so that all of the preconceived notions change with us?

This is the time of life to make a big difference in our years ahead and taking a look at how we are using our attitude in many areas of our lives and how attitude makes an impact on how we enjoy or not the last part of this miraculous existence.

What if just a few ways to look at how you are using your attitude can change your life for the better?

What if we worked with our thoughts so that they work for us to make a change for our greater good?

What if we took our attitude and designed it to bring more happiness, joy and peace to ourselves?

That is what this guide is for; to look at your attitude and how it can help you feel the best you ever have about yourself, your surroundings, your life in general, so the years ahead can be the best adventure of all.

CONTENTS

CHAPTER 1

What an Adventure this Journey called Life

"There is no map for the soul because we make it up as we go." – John Geddes

Adventure: an exciting or remarkable experience.

Wow, what an adventure it has been getting to the senior citizen stage of life!

It has been a remarkable trip with numerous paths taken, changing constantly, giving us so many different experiences to learn from.

We have made this journey called life by gaining wisdom as we go, using ingenuity, sheer willpower, and tenacity.

We should be very proud of ourselves as it may not have been as smooth as we might have liked it to be but we have made it this far, we are still here and we are still smiling (you are smiling aren't you?)

We have witnessed so many historical events that have changed our world and the way that we look at it. Technology has zoomed so fast that there are not enough words to cover it.

Isn't this the greatest time to be the senior citizens? There are so many adventures still ahead with so many advances in all areas of life so that it becomes easier and easier to go forward.

With all the technology we are able to communicate better, we are healthier with all of the advances in medicine, and we are certainly more informed about any and every subject you can think of.

We are the youngest looking, feeling and thinking senior generation to ever grace this planet. We are and always have been free thinkers so being those free thinkers why not make aging the biggest adventure of all?

Why not be very aware of how we use our thoughts and emotions in this stage of our lives and by being aware; how we can make it the best and happiest we have ever known?

Why not use our thoughts and emotions to our advantage so that we can be the most content, happiest and peaceful we have ever been?

Isn't it time to break the stereo-type that goes with senior citizen and bring to the title a whole new way of thinking about aging and how it is lived?

Let's create the proto-type for seniors that are upbeat, feeling great and living life to the fullest.

Why not be the senior generation that looks at aging in the best possible way?

If you look up the definition you will find what I mean about labeling those in their senior years. There are words like elderly, synonyms such as ancient, oldster, old-timer, golden-ager and of course elder.

There shouldn't be a label anymore for aging because we are not like the generations past; we are the new senior generation with all the advantages previous generations were not privy to, along with the awareness of positive thought.

Having these things and using them will make all future generations look at us as the senior generation that made aging easy, the age group which made it the exciting and remarkable time of life it can be.

We can change the label for aging to so much more than it has ever been.

We have changed things many things in our generation; there are many industries that have benefited from our sheer numbers and lifestyles. Wouldn't it be wonderful to change the way aging is perceived?

Each one of us has had many experiences on our own journey. It has been impacted by different situations and issues. Each person has dealt with their issues in their own way which is as it should be because we are all unique, have our own thought process, so there is no right way or wrong way there is each individual using their power of thought to make the journey as easy as they could for themselves.

Now that we are at this time in of our lives shouldn't we make the next 30 – 40 years the greatest we have ever known? Isn't it time to start enjoying everything that is around us and making it a point to start noticing and looking for the good things, the things that make life happy, fun and peaceful?

What would be the reason not too? Why would we not want to take these years ahead and use them for our greater good, to look at them in a softer and more lighthearted way? Why not let ourselves know the joy of just being and seeing life in the best possible way that we can?

We do have the power to do this you know, because we are unique and we have our own thought process we can make life as easy as we want to by using those thoughts in the most optimistic of ways.

We certainly don't want to be the stereotyped old men and women of yesteryear do we? Let's not, let's be the ones who change the way the older generation is supposed to be and show the world that growing older is a just mind over matter.

Let's make the adventure of aging the best it can possibly be with our own well-being at the very center of the best years of our lives.

Let's show the world that aging doesn't mean giving up and giving in to what others may think about getting older, let's prove that aging is about making the very most out of the years ahead of us.

The pages in this guide are to help you take a look at life and how we can choose to think and feel about who we are, where we have been, where we are now and where we are going in the best possible light.

Here is to a whole new way of making senior living the best it has ever been!

CHAPTER 2

This is about You

Our souls don't get older; they never wrinkle, wear out or tire.
They see life's beauty and hear the voice of conscience as clearly as ever.
And so, no matter how many years pass, each of us remains forever new inside.
And that is something to celebrate! – Anonymous

Celebration: to observe a notable occasion with festivities.

Life should be a celebration!

The first thing we should all celebrate that we are still here. I mean seriously we should celebrate this every day with a grin. It is a gift to still be here enjoying all life has to offer us.

We have survived the journey so far, some of us have had more bumps and bruises than others but we have all made it to this point.

We should celebrate the things we have accomplished, the fact that we have been a part of countless lives, and have had so many memorable experiences.

The celebration of our life is all about the very high points of our journey because these are the things that are important, that help us to feel good and are what celebrating is all about.

We can identify the times in our lives that may not have been the greatest but if we give them a moment's reflection we can appreciate them as learning experiences and also part of who we are now, what we like and do not like, so that we can look at them in a way that is not negative. These moments should be fleeting however because these are not what we want to use as a guideline for how we think about our lives.

Celebrations are happy times so these are the periods of our lives we should be remembering. There have been many more than we give credit to and unless we recognize them and give them the appreciation they deserve we are shortchanging the way we look at our lives.

There have been many highpoints for all of us in different ways; there are none that are the same because we are all very different in thoughts and feelings about living. So the celebration should be about you and the things along the way that were fulfilling for you, that brought you joy, and the acknowledgement that you did have important and satisfying times throughout your lifetime. These are the things to celebrate, to appreciate, to recognize.

Because the fact is; we are actually one of a kind, each one of us exceptional, it should help us realize that the life that we want to lead, how we want to be, relies solely on us. We are responsible for our own happiness and joy, and in fact, should not be looking anywhere else but inside ourselves.

We are important, each one of us, and the thing is, we should be our own first priority. At this stage of our lives, having come this far, if we don't understand that our happiness comes from inside us and nowhere else, then it is time to realize it and start using this knowledge to our advantage.

All of the most positive feelings come from within such as joy, peace, happiness, beauty, love. If we can use each one of these towards how we see ourselves, how we feel about who we are, then we can start feeling good about our lives and where we are at.

Throughout the years, the ups and downs, we have found out important things about ourselves. These things are important to who we are today and how we feel.

There is an *inner strength* in all of us that we have called upon and used over the course of our lifetime. If you take the time to think about your journey and how many times you have used this strength you will amaze yourself. When you do realize the times you used this strength you prove to yourself just by acknowledging it that is does exist and you are stronger than you thought you were.

We all have an extraordinary capacity for *love*, whether it is giving it or receiving it. Love is the foundation of all of us, it is what we all want most of all in our lives.

We at some point or another have had to use our *sense of humor* especially if times were a little difficult. Laughter is a great healer of the spirit.

We have cultivated a vast *wisdom* living life to this point that should be serving us well. Each of us have learned valuable lessons about living, about what makes us feel good and what we like. This wisdom is really about ourselves and how we function each day.

We all have experienced *joy* to the fullest in our life and know what that feels like. There is nothing like feeling the joy of things that make us uplifted and happy. We experience this in so many ways through so many avenues. Joy should be a priority for all of us.

We have all found within ourselves an inherent desire to seek and find happiness which is also a very central part of who we are. *Being happy* is first on everyone's list I am sure and it incorporates most of the things we have in our lives right now.

The reality that we have all of these traits and have used them is a good thing because if we recognize them, if we acknowledge them, they become a basis for us to work with as we go forward now to be all that we can be at this point of our lives.

By acknowledging that a great part of your life was about happiness and joy, and by knowing that you do in fact feel better when you are in this state of mind it makes sense to want to think and feel this way as much as you possibly can.

It is easy to fall back on unhappy thoughts or to cultivate them, for whatever reason they seem to stick out more than the happy ones if we allow them to, but we have all had happiness in our lives, we all choose happiness, so why not make that our focus and let go of anything that does not make us feel good.

It is kind of amazing don't you think to make a choice not to want to feel this way? If we are to use our thoughts to our best advantage then remembering the pleasure we have experienced is so important for us.

This is about you and your own well-being so switching from the negative to the positive in any line of thought can only enhance your way of living.

The first order of business here is to make your own life happy however that suits you.

By tapping into that, knowing how to feel happy, then you start bringing to yourself a way of life that is more enjoyable and satisfying.

Rely on yourself and your strength, love, humor, happiness and wisdom to bring into your life the peace and contentment you deserve at this moment and for the years ahead.

The fact is we are actually one of a kind, each one of us is unique and exceptional. So how you have experienced all of the emotions I just mentioned are just right for you. There is no mold to fill, no exact way to have felt what you felt. It is about you and your life and every one of us will have felt it differently, which in fact is great as this is what makes the world what it is.

There is no one person, situation, or place that can make us happy unless we choose to be happy. It is easy to blame people, places and things on an unhappy state of mind, but it is simply how we are choosing to look at all of these things and how we keep going over what was and is going on in our lives.

Our minds are like computers or for my friends who have yet to get a computer (you know you who are) files, that store all of experiences in our memory. Everything we have ever seen, heard or felt is stored there. We can pull these up anytime we choose to so utilizing the good ones, the ones that make us joyful are key to how we feel.

Just think about the memory of a computer and if it is too full it doesn't work as well as it should. It is slow-moving which impedes getting things done as quickly as you would like to. The first thing you do is start deleting files you don't use anymore, cleaning up and moving out things which are obsolete.

Your thoughts can be done the same way. Thoughts that do not serve you anymore that do not help you to feel good are ready, more than ready actually, to be deleted to make way for thoughts that can bring to you the well-being and peace that should be the goal of everyone in this age group.

If we are to make our lives a celebration, then we need to change our outlook to a more positive and uplifting way in which to see ourselves and everything around us.

We have so much life behind us, we are all very wise in so many areas of living, isn't it time we use this wisdom in our day to day being, to become even better and brighter than we ever have been before.

Have you every stopped and really thought about having an imagination? What would life be like if we didn't have one. It is pretty amazing when you think about it, because with every thought that we have we then have some kind of feeling with it and we immediately can bring up a picture in our mind clearly which goes with those thoughts and feelings. This is pretty potent don't you think, as there is not one person without the ability to imagine.

Put this to the test by first thinking of something that makes you happy, the first happy thought you have is fine. Then of course you have a picture in your mind and immediately you have a feeling to go with it. It is all very clear just like watching a movie and our memory bank is full of these happy thoughts and feelings.

We have experienced so many good times and good things and when we recognize all the enjoyment we have had throughout our lives, we can be aware of how many wonderful people, places and things we have had around us.

If we were not supposed to use our imagination we wouldn't have one so the question would be how are you using yours? Is it for the most positive experience or the most negative? Are you using yours to think and feel of times that brought happiness and joy or hurt you?

What would be the point do you think if we only used our thoughts and feelings in a negative way? To constantly think of the negative things in our past and present is to think of life as chore or a burden. Life is and can be so much more for us when we shed this way of thinking and bring to ourselves a whole new way to look at life, looking at the brightest spots not the darkest.

If we make a habit of bringing up the best thoughts to think and feel, thoughts that gratify us then we start to feel good and this would certainly be our goal. We can thrive in a way that feels good and makes every day just as easy and enjoyable as we would like.

At this stage of our lives we need to be in the now, right this minute, every minute of the day so that when we use our thought process this way, knowing we are looking at the best of life, seeing all that is good and beautiful around us, then we begin to appreciate who we are, where we are and how we want to proceed on this wonderful adventure.

This is all about you and how you want your life to be in the years ahead. Be kind to yourself and as you look forward now to making it the best part of the adventure know that you are fully capable of doing it just by paying attention to yourself and how you look at your life.

This is a generation of amazing caring individuals, so what if; we direct the rest of the adventure ahead and make it the very best part of our journey. It is time we truly start to celebrate our lives, reveling in the fact that we are here, we have made significant contributions to mankind whether they were large or small it does not matter and we still have so much contributing left to do.

This is the generation that should start a new label for being a senior citizen. How about we become the poster kids for aging and let everyone remember us as the shift in how to age with great technique.

Positive thoughts on reflecting on who you are:

- I choose to be as happy as I can possibly be.
- I have lived a good life and choose to recognize those times.
- I am a valuable person with strength and wisdom that has come with years of living.
- I will celebrate my life and how far I have come.
- I do know how to be happy because I have been many times over the years. I will use this to help me keep a happy feeling about myself and others.

CHAPTER 3

Attitude

"It isn't what you have or who you are or where you are or what you are doing that makes you happy or unhappy. It is what you think about it." – Dale Carnegie

Attitude: a state of mind or a feeling.

As we have aged, our attitude has done a little reshaping along with our bodies. We have gathered over the year's ideas, opinions, and knowledge which came to us in many different ways. Some of our life experiences have made definite impressions on us, some good and well some not so much.

Each experience has made a difference in how we look at things, how we react to situations and how we feel about certain aspects of our lives.

As I have said before we are each unique, like a snowflake if you will, not any one of us is the same. There is no one else like you in the world and that has some power to it in itself doesn't it?

Your attitude is strictly your own, it is about how you feel about yourself, your life, and every part of what goes on around you.

The way that you think and feel about yourself and your life is the most important thing about how you are caring for your well-being.

Here are some different words that describe emotions we each have experienced at one time or another which makes a difference in our attitude towards life and how we are feeling.

- Joy- a state of happiness
- Delight – a high degree of gratification
- Happy – enjoying well-being and contentment
- Considerate – thoughtful of the rights and feelings of others
- Compassion – sympathetic consciousness of others distress together with the desire to help alleviate it
- Worry – to afflict the mental distress or agitation
- Afraid – filled with fear and apprehension

- Anger – a strong feeling of displeasure or hostility
- Judgmental – a tendency to judge harshly
- Misery – a state of great unhappiness and emotional distress

When you read the words and definitions of all of the emotions or thought processes, it is easy to see which would make us feel the best that we can feel while the others could just pull us in a direction of not feeling as good as we could.

At the age we are now it is probably safe to say that we have a pattern of thought that influences the attitudes we have about life and all that goes on around us. Along with our attitudes there is a great amount of knowledge that we have gathered by living and learning.

We each have a definite way to think about things which is great because if we all thought the same way it would be a pretty boring world.

What if we took a look at the attitudes we are using on a daily basis and how these attitudes could make our lives as relaxed as they could be if we lightened up and started to soften our outlook on life.

Is it so very important for everyone to think in the same way? How would we even believe this is possible as each one of us has our very own thought process? Isn't it time to accept that we each have an idea of what life should be like and there is no wrong way just each person's own personal thoughts?

If you are always in turmoil because of the state of something you think should be a certain way and it isn't, does it make you feel good or not so good to keep that vein of thinking going?

At this stage of our lives, with the experiences we have had we should understand by now that there are so many different ways to achieve the same objective, there are so many different personalities that surround us, and life works differently for each and every person, so our attitudes about life should include accepting that there are different ways to do everything, different lifestyles for everyone and soften how we are looking at people, circumstances, and happenings.

What if we found one positive in everyone and everything we might not agree with? Then we let go of anything else negative we might think and feel. Think about it for just a moment and understand what a difference it would make to your well-being if you were to possibly change this just for the sake of making your years ahead peaceful.

If we are to be content in our time ahead, if we are to know a life of ease then it comes with taking a look at where our attitudes keep us in an emotional way. If we allow ourselves to relax and enjoy what is around us, what makes us happy, and let go of anything which doesn't do that a whole new world would open for us.

We want to feel the best that we can so if we lighten up a heavy attitude then we do start to feel better and better.

I am sure that you have been somewhere at sometime and witnessed a person that is very angry and expressing it in a very public way. You can see the waves of negativity spread out from them and surround the area that they are in. The anger vibrates doesn't it almost to the point of being tangible. You can see their unhappiness and it washes over everything in waves when it is publicly displayed.

On the other hand you probably have also seen someone who is laughing so hard there are tears in their eyes and they cannot get a grip and stop. You immediately smile because the vibration surrounding them is so positive and infectious you just can't help yourself. It is so uplifting to watch it seems that whenever we are around laughter of some kind there are always smiles and joy which makes us feel lighter in spirit just to listen to it.

Now that we are at this stage of our lives we have made choices galore, some good and well some not so good, but that is behind us now. Shouldn't this be the time of laughter in our lives, the time where things are fun and happy?

This is the point in life where we want to make the best choice about ourselves and how we feel. It is essential to feel good about who we are, where we have been and what we have done over our lifetime. It is also so very important to be happy about where we are right now.

This is the time now to make the choices of being happy and content, to know peace at its finest and to live our lives in a way that brings us the most beneficial time of life that we have ever known.

It doesn't have to do with the material but with the peace in our hearts and minds and the fact that we love the life we are living.

Here are some way to look at your attitude and its effect on you:

- ❖ How is my attitude affecting my daily life?
- ❖ How is my attitude affecting my health?
- ❖ Would softening my attitude help me?
- ❖ How would I feel better if I changed my attitude to a more positive outlook?
- ❖ How could I change the attitude of controlling everything?

When you take the time to think about how your attitude affects you and you begin ways to soften it and lighten up you will feel the difference in your well-being. You will feel different in a way that will be distinctly yours for your greater good.

Positive thoughts on a lighter attitude:

- I know everyone does not feel the same way that I do about life and that is okay.
- I want to see only the finest things in my life every day and when I do I feel the best I have ever felt.
- I want to let go of judging others because they don't think like I do.
- Life is an adventure for me and I look forward to it every day.
- I will make the effort to laugh and be more lighthearted during the day.
- I want my attitude to be the best that it can be so that I make this part of my life the best part of my journey.

CHAPTER 4

Appreciation for Who You Are

Life is not about finding yourself, it is about creating yourself – George Bernard Shaw

Accomplishment: something completed successfully – an achievement.
Appreciation: an ability to understand the worth, quality, or importance of something.

This now is the phase of life where you can take a look back appreciate all of the things that you have accomplished in your lifetime so far. You have done many positive things and you need to take the time to recognize them and appreciate them.

If you have a habit of thinking about some of the worst things in your life *don't*.

Why is it do you suppose that when we look back at our lives we tend to make our mistakes and heartaches the most important things that stand out in our minds? They just pop up and are larger than life when in fact we have done so much more than those instances.

Again our imaginations just go full bore on what went wrong or was wrong, when in fact, there were so many things that went right and were right that they supersede all that was negative. We just have to recognize this fact and believe it.

Really and truly kids, there were so many more things that went right in our lives that we need to make a herculean effort to bring those up in our thoughts and allow them to help us become more of a positive thinker than we have ever been.

Value all that you are, by doing this you acknowledge that you are a very important part of mankind, of the planet and have brought something important to all of us just by being who you are. All of the times you showed kindness, caring and compassion throughout the years has made a difference so acknowledging these are just stepping stones to all the other things you have accomplished.

Take this time also to realize that you did the best you could with what you knew at each moment you have lived. You were basically just being the best person you could be with the knowledge of life that you had at the time.

When I sat down and started thinking about what I have done over the years between raising kids, being a housewife, and all of the activities the kids were involved in, then working outside of the home later in life I was amazed at all I had done.

If you need to sit and make a list of all of the good things you have done and have accomplished by all means do so. You might find it most helpful because once you start writing and you concentrate on all of the positive things that have happened to you more and more come to mind once you begin.

By making a list it is tangible and it also verifies that you did accomplish many things. Start out with the simplest of accomplishments and soon you will realize that they just get bigger and bigger as you remember what was.

There should be no criticism here of any kind because if you hadn't made any mistakes along the way you wouldn't have been living, you would have just been existing. Remember none of us are perfect and the journey we have been on is one of learning about ourselves and who we are.

By living life to the fullest there will be some blips on the screen but if you take a look at what you consider a hard time or a mistake you will find that if in fact it didn't occur you might not be where you are now or who you are with.

Make sure that you are your own cheerleader and you make all the things you bring up good and happy and joyful. What has gone right in your life is what you should be concentrating on and you will find once you start paying attention to what has over the years been good you will find that life has been a pleasurable experience.

This is our time now, right where we are and by bringing all of the positive aspects of our lives from the past we can feel good about continuing forward with our knowledge and insight, knowing that we did in fact have many good experiences, happy times, fun events, so that we can be the very best we have ever been in the way that we think and feel about life's journey ahead.

You not only find that you have had many great and happy times but you also realize that you are completely capable of being in that state of mind when you choose to. You have felt all the good feelings that came with all the great experiences you recall so use those feelings to your greatest advantage.

Once you have a good feeling about who you are just by acknowledging things you have accomplished and done you have just proven that your thoughts are very important to how you feel.

This is a major attitude adjustment for the better. This is about bringing yourself to at state of well-being by the illumination that you are and always have been guided by the attitude you have about yourself and about life.

Remember that attitude is a state of mind so if you choose to make yours the best it can be about all that you are and all that is going on around you then you will make aging a piece of cake.

This is your starting point of change for the better by making the effort to focus on what you appreciate about who you are and the positive feelings you have about yourself when you realize that you have in reality had great times with people, situations and life in general, that you have accomplished more that you thought you did which makes you understand you are a remarkable person.

Life has been good if you choose to see it that way and why wouldn't you want to?

Positive thoughts on appreciation of self:

- I realize I have had great times in my life.
- I choose to think kind and loving thoughts about my life.
- I have done positive things in my life that have made me appreciate who I am.
- I have had fun in my life and when I think about those times it makes me smile and feel good.
- I love my personality and what I have to offer mankind.
- I have accomplished so many things and I am ready to accomplish even more.

CHAPTER 5

Choices and Changes

*"Just because something is ingrained in you doesn't make it true.
Remember, we once believed the world was flat." – Louise Hay*

Choose: to select from a number of possible alternatives.
Change: to cause to be different.

We all know the importance of choices as we have made many over the years. Some we are very happy that we did make, others, well enough said.

The thing is choices are a part of the person we are and they make up a large part of what has happened to us as we made our way to this point. We have all tried, still do for that matter, to choose wisely but sometimes we don't and that is all a part of the life experience. With all of the practice at life that we have had we understand now how important it is to choose what feels right for us.

We do have in our power at this time of our life to choose how we use our thoughts; where we focus, and to tune into the feelings that come with those thoughts.

I am sure we are all searching for ways to feel good, to be in the best place mentally and physically, so the question here is: are we stuck in the same place spinning our wheels or are we moving forward to the place that would bring us the best well-being possible.

When we use our thoughts and feelings together to focus on anything it then determines how we feel. When you were focused on your accomplishments weren't the feelings you had uplifting to you, didn't you feel positive about what has come before you? Didn't you feel a strong feeling of self worth?

All thoughts and feelings are linked to each other, so it is about how we choose to use them, how we choose to make them work for us, and how we choose to understand how they benefit our well-being.

Let's just say for the sake of argument you thought of something that wasn't very happy about your life. When those thoughts surfaced the feelings attached to them were not so good were they? Those thoughts are a way to show you that if you in fact want to feel good, be upbeat and happy then the choice of thoughts is of major importance to you.

Our choice to think the best thoughts possible about all areas of our lives is the greatest way for us to see results in our well-being.

Here is a list of ideas that may help in looking at choices and change:

❖ What areas of my life could I make the choice to change for my greater good?
❖ How can I change my thoughts to the more positive side of my life?
❖ Where in my life can changing my attitude and focusing my thoughts make a difference?
❖ What part of my life would improve by changing my thoughts to the most positive they can be towards it?
❖ If my outlook changed to be more positive where would I start?

It is about how we focus on all of the areas of our lives and how this affects us if we are not choosing to keep thoughts and feelings that help us stay in the positive.

I will tell you that choice and change are two of the most powerful things you can do for yourself because once you become aware of what your focus is, how you are thinking and feeling by using this focus, you have the ability to control where you are mentally, physically and spiritually.

I know each one of us want only the best years ahead of us so making a habit of seeing the good things in your life and all around you is a great way to start feeling the very best that you can.

Isn't it time to choose to soften our attitudes, to choose to change our thoughts to be optimistic instead pessimistic? Isn't it time to choose to change anything that would hinder our well-being?

Each person is valuable and it is time for all of us to see our own value and to love who we are. We have put so much energy into our lives to get where we are right now so the important thing here is to choose to change the feelings we have about ourselves to the very best they can be.

Change is not a word that is associated with senior citizens, I am sure that every senior group has felt this way but isn't it time to make a difference and be the senior citizen generation that is willing to make a change for the better in the way their attitudes make a profound difference in who they are, how they feel, and how they live ?

When we choose to change our thinking from what is wrong around us to what is right we start to notice how much better we feel, how many things are pleasing to us and how much our attitude in this direction makes a difference in our lives.

Why not be the senior generation that changes geriatric thinking for the healthier both mentally and physically? Why not choose to be the generation that starts looking at things in the brightest light possible?

We can stay in the stereotype of aging, listening to what others tell us we are going to act like, feel like or be like. That would be easy to fall into wouldn't it?

Why not be in charge of how you want aging to be for yourself? If we choose to be our own generation of aging and we change how we are looking at our lives to the most positive way possible then we do make the difference in daily life for ourselves.

This of course is a choice, but when you think about it why not be the best thinking generation on the planet? Why not be the change in yourself that leads to better health in every aspect of life?

Positive thoughts on choosing and changing:

- I choose to think in the most positive way that I can.
- I want to change my outlook to the best it can be.
- I know by changing my attitude for the better I see life at its best.
- Change makes life more interesting.
- I am willing to make the choice to look at change in the areas of my life that will do the most good.
- I am not afraid of change when it is for the positive and I feel so much better doing it.

CHAPTER 6

Focus

"Find your focus by seeking all that is good in your life." — Lorii Myers

Focus: a center of interest or activity

As we have been discussing, all thoughts are linked to feelings, which in turn create our focus. If we want our lives, our surroundings and even the world to be a better place, a place that is peaceful and enjoyable then it would make sense to start within ourselves.

Where is your attention focused on during the day? What are you using to center yourself and your life so that you feel good? Isn't it time for each of us to center ourselves so contentment with who we are, where we are and what we are doing is our main focus?

It does take practice because all of us being human, and possibly practicing being critical or cynical in some areas of our lives, we have formed some unhappy habits of negativity.

It takes work to turn that attitude and focus around but it is well worth the effort to do so and not as hard as you might think.

Once you start doing it you notice the difference in how you feel physically and mentally and it makes the process of changing your focus to the positive so much easier.

I have had many conversations with people about why it is that we tend to think about the negative things first and expound on them when they don't really make us feel good and the consensus is it is a habit and because of this that is where the focus is.

The thing is most of the time we are not even aware we are being negative because we are so used to the feelings and the conversations they are just routine. Before you know it one negative thought starts and it sends our focus in a direction that is not in our best interest.

Life is just too great to be wasted on feeling negative and focusing on those types of thoughts.

Believe it or not there are as many if not more, good things that happen constantly in your life, in your surroundings and in the world. If we choose to start a habit of looking for those things, believing that there is more good than bad, allowing ourselves to start focusing on the beauty of our lives, the lives around us and the world in general, a sense of peace and contentment would be the biggest part of who we are.

I would challenge you to start your day in a way that brings the good things to the forefront of your thoughts. This is where choosing to change the way that we are focusing on our lives is an enormous step to the most positive way to live.

There are so many things you can focus on about your life and your surroundings that make you feel good it is worth the endeavor.

If you would like to you can track all of the good and positive things that happen during your days. Here is a way to do it that is easy and quick:

You will need a basket, bowl or jar that will hold several pieces of paper. Start out on the first day of the month writing something positive that happened to you during the day. Even if the day was not one of your best think of something good that happened and write it down. Do this each day of the month. Make a practice at the end of the day to think of something that made you feel good and make a note of it. On the last day of the month sit down and read all of the things that were positive in your life. You will see at the end of the month there are so many positive things that have happened which helped you to feel upbeat. Start again at the beginning of a new month and you will find yourself looking for things to note every day but most importantly you will be aware of how many good things happen during a day's time.

When we start appreciating all the things that make us feel good when we think of them, or can see them then we begin expanding what is right in our lives because once we start that type of focus then more and more things become apparent to us that we may have been taking for granted or missing altogether.

It is like a light goes on which illuminate more and more of the good things that make up who you are, where you are and what you are doing. It is worth the endeavor to bring into focus what feels good to you, what brings you satisfaction and what shows you that you can feel this way just by observing.

Cynicism is a detrimental way to feel about life. If we carry this negativity with us it is like a weight that pulls us down because we just can't feel as good as we could if we weren't bogged down in such pessimism.

I am sure you feel you have reasons for a cynical attitude but let me assure you that it is hurting you more than it is helping you. If you would let go of it bit by bit you will find that you feel lighter and better and things start to ease up for you when you finally let it all go.

If you are being very hard on yourself, if you are looking at your life in a negative way then you are robbing yourself of feeling as good as you can. This is about *your* life now, it is important that your focus be on all of the good things that are within you as well as around you.

The glass half empty and the glass half full has been around forever but it is really in how you are focusing on all things that draw your attention. If you attention is drawn to the glass half empty then you are shortchanging yourself.

This is about right now, this minute, things to be thankful for, things that are right and things that make us feel the best we can in our hearts and minds.

Give yourself a break will you, celebrate that you are in this moment living and breathing so that the gift of life is all yours to do with as you choose to, to focus on the best there is, and to feel the finest you have ever felt.

It is your right to feel good, it is your right to take care of yourself and it is most definitely your right to be happy.

Here are some things you might focus on to help you keep in a positive frame of mind:

- Love of Family
- Nature
- Music
- Pets
- Garden
- Hobbies
- Friendships

I am sure that you have many more that can go here, add whatever you feel you could use your focus on in your life these are just suggestions for you, everyone has so many different things that fulfill their lives and whatever does for you is right.

CHAPTER 7

Revamping our Focus

*"For every minute you are angry you lose 60 seconds
of happiness." – Ralph Waldo Emerson*

Revamping: to make something better or like new again.

If you could change your focus so that you felt better, energized, and content where would you start?

Here are things to focus on which will strengthen your life.

- ❖ Love of Self
- ❖ Forgiveness
- ❖ Compassion
- ❖ Non-Judgment
- ❖ Encouragement

Here are things to let go of so that your focus is the best it can be:

- ❖ Anger
- ❖ Hate
- ❖ Criticism
- ❖ Self Doubt
- ❖ Grudges

Using our focus for our greater good brings to each of us better health, happier feelings, and a much easier way to think.

Our age is only a number, it does it does not define us; it is how we think that defines us. Let's not let ourselves be stereotyped into an age group that are so set in their ways they we are bitter and grouchy, let's be the generation who will change the very look and feel of the geriatric set.

I am sure that we can all bring up a memory of someone in our lives that was elderly and was difficult because they would not change their way of thinking and wanted to stay in the same place thought wise which made their life more difficult than it needed to be. Their focus was on what *was* so they missed out on what was good in their later life.

Let them be an inspiration to us to have the ability to choose to change and become better with age and to be more in the know of how to think more positively and go forward with greater ease than they did.

If we choose not to be narrow minded, if we can be open to change and allow ourselves to live in the moment for all its worth, then there is an easiness about life that brings us a feeling of contentment and peace. I am sure that each of us wants this for ourselves more now than ever before.

Positive thoughts on revamping our focus:

- I am choosing what I focus on every morning so that I feel the best I can feel.
- My focus is important to me so I choose to direct it in ways that help my well-being.
- When I focus it is like using binoculars, I zoom in on the good things happening around me.
- My focus is a tool for me to feel the best I possibly can.

There are several areas of our lives we focus on that can be revamped. These areas have affected all of us and may still be doing so in which case recognizing that change is necessary so that we do have an era of ease about our life

Let's take a look at what they are.

CHAPTER 8

The Past is called History

"Never let your past experiences harm your future. Your past can't be undone and your future doesn't deserve the punishment." – Anonymous

Past: having existed in the time before the present.

If you could start with a clean slate right here and right now, if you could clear your mind and be ready to go forward using positive thoughts as your foundation where would you start?

The past is a place we all like to visit once and a while. Visit is the key word here as we certainly don't want to make it the place we think about all of the time. We do however like to go back and refresh our memories of times gone by and that is okay if we are thinking about all of those good times we had.

However, it is much more important that we are living in the now, in this moment and that we start each day with thoughts that keep us in the best state of mind we can have. So if we consider this a clean slate and we are using our focus to only feel good then the past has no place here unless we use it for positive thoughts.

We have addressed the habit of negative focusing and the past is a place if we let it where we might bring up things that are not for our greater good.

There is no fun in talking about what went wrong in your life, who has made you unhappy, or any other negative situation that has been lived. It is kind of like have a needle stuck on a vinyl record. You remember how records were, the needle would stick and wear a groove in the record and then it would never go past that part of the song, it would just keep playing it over and over again.

I am sure that every one of us want to make this the most fun and the most enjoyable part of our lives and to do this those places that we have been stuck on that were negative and unhappy from our past need to be replaced with what was right in your life, the people who have made you the happiest, the things that you have done that have been great and all that was good which helped make you who you are today.

Now is the time to let go of whatever has worn a groove into your life that was negative and keeps coming around and around. It simply doesn't matter how long ago it was or how big it was it is history. It is serving no purpose at all

By letting go of that constant loop of thought that brings you unhappiness, you then stop the feelings of hurt, anger or sadness which are destructive to your incredible spirit. Just let all of those negative loops from the past go, stop allowing them to bring you to a place that no longer exists, a place that is all air and space and should be faded away by now.

Past experiences can bring on cynicism, and as we have discussed, is not in our best interest. If because of past experience we see only the worst in life, in people, in the world then we are not giving ourselves the opportunity to be as happy as we could be, to feel the best we can feel and to make our lives as balanced as they can be.

If we were to stop being pessimistic, if we let go of anger and all the feelings that go with it because of a past negative experience, then we begin to loosen up and start feeling the ease in life which is how it should be.

When we let go of the past and anything that was unhappy, we start to soften our thoughts, we can if we choose to see the good in everything, people, places, situations, and this starts a very simple change within our thought process. It makes such a difference for our way of life because we can start really enjoying our journey, appreciating life, and being at peace in our years ahead.

What if we let go of any unhappiness about what *was* in our lives but look at what is right *here* and *now* in a brighter light so that all of our tomorrows are the brightest they can be.

When you begin to think of something that is negative in your past make the choice to change that thought to something more positive. It is our choice about what we think, so if we make the conscious effort to change what we are thinking from the negative to the positive then we control how we feel.

We have discussed choosing and changing and here is a very important part of life to use those two things for your greater good. We can choose to not dwell on anything in our lives from the past and in turn we change our direction of thought to a place that suits us and our positive thinking.

When we are free of the burden of carrying around past issues we give ourselves permission to go forward with the intention of bringing happiness to our thoughts and this begins a cycle of treating ourselves to the life we deserve, one of peace and pleasure.

When you free yourself from negativity you let yourself become someone who enjoys the life you are living to the fullest. Just think of the entire he said, she said, they did, they didn't do, stuff that you carry around with you all of the time that serves no purpose whatsoever but to weigh you down.

It is simply a matter of choosing to change this focus on what was past and zooming in on what is now, and how good it is for you no matter what transpired before. If we can consciously make this choice to stop rehashing what was whenever it happened then we can talk about the great things that are going on right now for us with a better feeling about life in general.

Let's not let the past put a twist in our now, let's just give ourselves the best way of thinking possible and go forward with anticipation of just the greatest well-being achievable.

What can you let go of from the past that will benefit you?

- ❖ Childhood experiences at home or at school
- ❖ Relationships that did not work out
- ❖ Employment that was not satisfactory
- ❖ Family Issues

You will have more I know I just hit a few places where we all have had situations that can fit here. Take the time to think about what you could let go of that would help you to feel better and better because it is no longer a part of your focus.

Unburden yourself by allowing those things that may still weigh on you to leave your thoughts. Picture yourself free of having to carry them around any longer.

Positive thoughts on leaving the past behind:

- I choose to not let my past rule my future.
- What can I let go of today from my past that will help me feel better?
- I see the past as a learning experience so that I pick out all of the positive things that came from all of my experiences.
- My past is part of who I am today and I will use only the most positive parts of it to benefit from.
- I am letting go of a negative thought about my past that does not affect me anymore.
- I choose to let go of all thoughts from my past that are uncomfortable and choose to bring up some of my happiest moments in my life
- I am letting go any issue from my past that I have allowed to interfere with my well-being.

CHAPTER 9

Letting Go

*"The beautiful journey of today can only begin when we
learn to let go of yesterday." – Steve Maraboli*

*"Holding on to anger is like drinking poison and
expecting the other person to die." – Buddha*

Let go: to relax one's hold on.

Habit: a usual way of behaving: something a person does often and in a regular repeated way.

Don't Look Back......You Aren't Going That Way

We have covered the fact that the past is what was and life today is what is, so the idea here now is the letting go of what was so you can be the person you want to be now, the one that does not allow negative issues to hold back happiness.

However, I know from personal experience, working with clients, and conversing with others in our age group, that nine times out of ten we are still focused on one or more things in our past that were either hurtful or have made us angry.

The stories we tell about the past are just as real as if they happened yesterday instead of many years before. They still haunt us, upset us, and still bring upheaval whenever we discuss them.

The fact is the more we keep reliving these experiences, the more we talk about them, bring them back to life, the negativity of them grows larger and larger even though they are old and tired.

They are like echoes we shout out about something negative and the negativity comes back at us over and over. They are not real we just keep them going by shouting out. If we quiet whatever it is we have been shouting about then we don't have the repeating negative feelings.

Imagine what your life would be like if you did not have sad, angry, hurtful moments in your past. They of course were there for a purpose, to let us find out what we want and don't want in our lives, and now since we have realized these points this would be the time to let each one of those go so we can concentrate on ourselves, on happiness, contentment, and well-being.

It is really time don't you think to let go of all of the things that adversely affect your beautiful spirit. Whether it was forty years ago or last week this is about beginning to heal all that hurts or angers and making life the best it can be for the rest of the years we are here.

This is no different than getting a diagnosis about your physical health. If you were told your blood pressure is too high then you would look into what it would take to lower it wouldn't you?

You should want to let go of anything negative in your thoughts and feelings for your greater good, so that you can be enjoying wonderful emotional health.

What makes negative thoughts any different for your well-being than any physical ailment you might have? If you are striving for a better feeling life then letting go of things that drag you down emotionally is key here to achieving that.

By letting go and realizing what wasted energy we are using by reliving unhappiness in our lives whenever it may have occurred, by not allowing those circumstances, people or issues to really be a thing of the past that can no longer touch us in a way that hurts our well being, then we take charge of feeling as good as we possibly can.

Here is a news flash for you: all of those you may have issues with are going on with their own lives or may no longer be alive, it is you who are in turmoil and are allowing negativity to interfere with being all you would be. It would be you who is allowing yourself to be twisted and turned in a direction that is not in your own best interest.

Let's not inflict anymore painful thoughts about what was on ourselves, let's instead move forward with a whole new attitude choosing to change what we are focusing on when we are thinking about our life, making sure that it is the most positive focus we can have.

If you decided to clean out your medicine cabinet at home of prescriptions and over the counter meds you have stored there, the first thing you would look at it the expiration date on them. If you found some that were outdated, you would get rid of them for the fact that they are no longer useful, or they could possibly be harmful. It is ongoing that we have newer and better medication all of the time which benefits those that have to take it.

How about we start using newer and better thoughts about ourselves where we are and how we are feeling? I would ask you to take a look at some of the negative issues that still kept going around and around in your head for a moment and have you check the dates on them. Some of them have expired so long ago they must have whiskers.

Isn't it time to get rid of those because they are harmful to you in a way that can hurt you as you keep reliving them by thinking or speaking of the subject?

If you think about it, when you are rolling those negative thoughts around in your head how do you feel? Are the feelings that come over you ones you want to live with? Are the thoughts that follow one after another in a negative way helping your well-being or are they harmful to it?

If we let go of these unconstructive thoughts and emotions our future is looking brighter because we are in control of how we focus on what is right now and what was once upon a time truly becomes the past.

One of the things to wrap your thoughts around is this: People are always doing the best they know how to do at each time of their lives. You, me and everyone you know, in fact everyone in the world is doing the best that they can.

Anyone can stay the same doing the same things over and over it is all about choice. It is your choice to change the way you see and think about any situation and let go of anything negative about it.

If in fact we are going to celebrate our time here and how far we have already come then our focus is on only who we are right now, the good things all around us, and the happiness and joy we have experienced on this journey.

We do know how to feel happy, we have felt this way so many times in so many different situations over the years that it is not hard to do if we in fact make it a habit to be in that frame of mind.

When we let go of the unhappy times and embrace the happy ones it shifts our perspective our attitude and our focus so that our life becomes one of joy and serenity.

There are two things we can learn to let go of which helps our focus immensely. These two things are ingrained in our daily thought process more than most of us would like to admit and you will know them immediately.

Being in control and being right.

About this control thing, it is a very wise person who realizes that we just do not need to control anything except where our thought process is at. By letting go of control and just allowing life to flow we are then able to see the bigger picture of everything around us and it may surprise you to see how amazing it is when you stop trying to dictate the direction things are going. You know there is a difference in being prepared and controlling everyone and everything.

The first thing to really pay attention to is that most people do not think alike in every single instance. Good for us because it would be an incredibly dull world and needless to say we would all be doing the same thing.

If we respect the fact that not everyone thinks like we do, does things the same way or wants the same things we do; then it becomes apparent that we should just take care of ourselves, our own environment, so that life runs smoothly for us.

Our energy should be about peace and contentment in our own lives and let others do what they do to achieve it for themselves.

I am sure that this is a difficult thing to read for several, as some of us are control freaks and we just can't help ourselves. But if you analyze how controlling makes you feel just for a moment you will understand how tough it really is to expend all of that power on so many things that could very well be out of your control anyway.

It is exhausting to try to keep all the oranges in the air at one time isn't it? Why not just relax and see your life as easy and peaceful and let everyone else juggle their own oranges.

When we use our focus on ourselves then our time is well spent just seeing to our own needs and wants. That frees up everyone else to do their thing and isn't that calming already?

Take if from a reformed controller, it is so worth letting go, relaxing into life and knowing that you will feel so much better when you do.

What is the worst thing that can happen by letting go of control, of just letting everything and everyone be what they are? Could it be a whole new outlook on life, could it be an ease of your thoughts so that you can enjoy being without these interruptions? Sounds pretty scary…..not!

If we try to control everything, try to make sure things go a certain way we may be inhibiting something better from coming into our lives. Sometimes it just helps to let go and see how things line up.

Being in control and being right go hand in hand. This is a tough one because we have all had so many years of needing to be right. The one question you must ask yourself is this; "Is it worth it?"

So much negative energy is expended because someone has to be right. In fact if you take a look at some of the issues in your life you will find they are based on the fact that you think you are right and they think they are right. Chaos can be the result.

Isn't it better to agree to disagree so that life stays easy and peaceful?

There comes a time when we could adjust our thinking on being right and how we handle it so that we can again, let go and just be the person we are right now today and let everyone else be the same. If you are taking care of how you think and feel and where your focus is then you know what is right for you and that is all that matters.

Now I hope you are all not gasping for breath here as that is not my intention. It is my intention to ask you to take a look at how important these things are to you and to lighten up so that they are not the most central thing in your thought process.

Let go of the criticism of life issues, people, and situations. Remember that each of us has our own thought process and what is right for one may not be right for the other.

It is important to understand that if we do not know about another's life then how could we possibly be critical of how they are living it. When we let go of judging everyone else to the standard we expect in life then things lighten up. It is a pretty heavy load we carry around if we think we have all the answers to everyone else's life.

This of course takes practice, but you can do it and when you do you will feel the difference in your day to day existence because you will only be thinking about what is good for you and how you are going to focus for yourself.

There is power in that alone don't you think?

Positive thoughts on letting go:

- What will I choose to let go of today that will help me feel better?
- I choose to let go of anything negative that holds me back from being the best feeling person I can be.
- I choose to let go of any negative emotion no matter how long ago it was I experienced it so that I can feel the freedom that gives me.
- I choose to let go of controlling anything but myself. I will try as hard as I can to let others live their lives as they wish to.
- I choose to listen to others and agree to disagree with love.
- What area of my life have I spent enough negative energy on that I am ready to let go of?
- I choose to only control the remote for the television.

CHAPTER 10

Love of Self

*"Yesterday I was clever, so I wanted to change the world. Today
I am wise, so I am changing myself." – Rumi*

*"To love a person is to see all of their magic, and to remind
them of it when they have forgotten." -Unknown*

Love: a feeling of strong or constant affection for a person.

We are individuals that are made to love. We give and receive love constantly daily so it is very much a part of us. With just a thought of someone or something the feeling of love just blooms within our heart.

This love we have inside which we have shared with so many needs to be channeled inward to ourselves first so that the feeling of it brings each of us the same joy that we feel when we give it to others.

As the quote above says look for *your magic, remind yourself* whenever you need to that you are a great person with so many excellent qualities.

Remember as often as you can during the day all of the things you love about yourself. Take the time to recognize the traits about yourself that make you feel good.

If we care about ourselves first it makes caring for others so much more powerful because we are in tune with the mind-set of giving and receiving love.

We have over the years given so much to others without thinking about what we may need just from ourselves. If we put our needs as most important then we begin to be satisfied with more of life and all that we do. It is not wrong to think of yourself first, if you ponder that for a moment and realize that when you do this you are in a better frame of mind therefore life is much easier.

We really need to acknowledge that we are each a unique, beautiful spirit that has done the very best that they could do over the years. We need to understand that there is no one else like us on the planet, that our thoughts and feelings are ours alone and it make us vastly important to the human race and everyone that surrounds us.

It is time to stop beating yourself up or anyone else for that matter about anything negative that happened in your life because when you want your frame of mind to be on contentment, you cannot still be berating yourself or others as this tends to be a bummer and brings only discontent to your thoughts and your well-being.

If you have ever loved unconditionally in your life then you know the free feeling of that. It is time to apply that to *you* and just love yourself no matter what has gone on before this point in time.

Unconditional love is one that overlooks flaws and mistakes. Isn't it time you started overlooking those that you perceive of yourself and start looking at yourself with a more positive and inspiring attitude?

Isn't it time to forgive and forget all that went on behind us and look towards our future with anticipation because we have changed our attitude about ourselves as we begin caring about who we are, what we think and what we feel?

So many people talk about their Bucket List and what they want to achieve during their lifetime. The first thing on anyone's list should be validating all of the happy and fulfilling times they already have had throughout their journey. Start from the beginning and take each high point as you have grown as a person so that you have a tremendous highlight reel of your life in your thoughts to show you that life has been pretty great.

Take the time to look at who you are, how far you have come and the strengths that you have. Take a look at the things that you do really well and have done over the years. There are many more things you do well than you don't.

Love yourself for the person you are today and remember that you did the very best you could do throughout your life with the self-knowledge you had at the time.

You know at this stage of life the most important thing is not how we look on the outside it is how we feel on the inside. We should be celebrating our life not caring what other people think, what other people have, or what other people do.

We should concentrate on what makes us the most happy. We surely have that one down by now, we certainly know what makes us happy and what does not so our purpose now is to feel the happiest we have ever felt so that what we feel inside is love of self and who we are.

It is time now to be doing what makes us happy, what feels good and what is fun. It can be as simple as playing with your pet, gardening, having coffee with friends, or enjoying a hobby. The simplest things are sometimes the most pleasurable

It is feeling good that is the main objective here, the day to day looking for and doing things that just make life excellent.

It should be our intention to enjoy the upcoming years so it means we have to give ourselves permission to do that by understanding it is for our greater good to let go and let the love of self, who we are today be the focus that helps us to be centered for the next leg of our journey.

When we love ourselves we make the effort to take care of ourselves, it is worth it to take the time to show that we in fact do care about who we are and are proud of our age.

Make the effort everyday to look your best; you will feel even better when you do this. Each of us has our own style so however you do this is just right for you. Be yourself, look your best and you will find that your attitude is upbeat as well. Once we get going and do this we become energized and we feel great.

When we love ourselves we are aware of our health and make the effort to be in good physical condition all of the time. You know what is best for you as we are all different and there are so many diverse ways to attain this. Aren't we fortunate to have the technology and medicines available to help us have the very best possible health and welfare?

You are a beautiful spirit, one of a kind, and you have so much more to contribute to everyone around you so look for all that is good about yourself and love who you are because there isn't anyone else like you so it is your job to live out your life with great confidence.

Be an example of aging with style and grace by loving yourself, how you look and your well-being.

Positive thoughts on self-love:

- I love my strength of character
- I love my kindness and sense of compassion.
- I love my sense of humor and how I make people laugh.
- I love the way I see so much beauty around me.
- I love who I am today and every day.
- I love the person I evolved into after all these years.

CHAPTER 11

Family Dynamics

"Happiness is having a large, loving, caring, close-knit family in another city." – George Burns

Family: a group of people that are related to each other.

The quote is a humorous one but does fit some of our lifestyles. As we have aged our family dynamics have changed over the years so there are many different scenarios going on in everyone's lives.

Each one of us has had specific experiences called family which has shaped us along with our attitudes over the years. We of course have made our own way and become the adults we have chosen to become but we have now and did have at one time definite input by family experiences.

Childhood started this whole thing going. There are so many scenarios here it is probably a whole other book, but some are still struggling with issues from there so let's touch a bit on that part of our lives. We are much more than our childhood years; they were a very short yet very influential part of our lives; however we as adults made choices and changes that helped us to become who we are today.

Childhood is where we learned a few things about the positives and negatives of life. We have carried some of that with us through the years but being individuals we have cultivated so much more on our own.

We learned behavior patterns in childhood and expounded on them as adults, so here we are at this stage with family experiences to talk about and remember, and to recognize the fact that we are products of that but are so much more because we learned additional lessons about life as we aged and changed.

Everyone has different tales to tell about childhood and if they are not happy ones then it is time to re-evaluate how detrimental they are to us if in fact we keep bringing them up and thinking about them.

It is easy to figure out the difference between telling a happy or not so happy story about your childhood and how it makes you feel. There is nothing better than a story that ends in laughter and nothing worse than one that brings you the feeling of misery.

Doesn't it make sense to let go of any thought that becomes a story of unhappiness? If we are to feel the best we can possibly feel then we must think about ourselves and what carrying around all of this old baggage is doing to our welfare

If we are replaying these unhappy moments in our thoughts, if we are repeating them in stories about what was, something that is old and over with, then we take on that negativity, we take ourselves back to that time and relive it.

Every time we do this we are not allowing ourselves to let go of these experiences which then hurts our well-being. By doing this we take several steps backwards instead of going forward like we want to.

It should always be validated when people experienced things in their youth that should not have happened to children, it should never be acted as if it did not. Everyone is important and valuable so validation that it was wrong is important.

Once it is addressed please understand that it is not helping you to relive it or talk about it. If you start to let go of it knowing that you do not want it to interfere with your life in this moment you free up your mind to think about things that are happening now that bring you joy.

At this point in our life that child that we were wants more than anything to be the grown adult that we are right now with the ability to use our thoughts to make our life relaxed and cheerful.

If we choose to no longer allow ourselves to be caught up with thoughts of a time so long ago, a time when we were not able to help ourselves because of our age, we can after all these years make a positive move so that our senior years will benefit greatly because we made this choice.

By changing your attitude about *what was* you begin a whole new attitude about *what is* in a much better frame of mind.

Letting go is especially important about this phase of life if you need to. Some of the memories are old and withered and ready to be gone if you will permit them to.

It is the now that we should be focused on, exactly where we are and be ready to live the best years of our lives.

Positive thoughts on childhood.

- I chose to look back at my childhood for only the happy times I spent there.
- I love who I am now and the child that I was helped me to get here.
- Anything in my childhood that I choose to let go of fades away easily.
- I choose to live in this moment with great love for myself.

Family was the beginning of our socialization and learning experiences. It is a force of energy that has been either positive or negative given the situations or issues that arise in this dynamic throughout the years.

If we are to feel the best that we possibly can then it is best to take a positive outlook at our family no matter what the situation is.

Keep in mind this is about choice, change and letting go so that our attitude makes a difference for us and our well-being.

I am in no way advocating that anyone fix anything as far as family relationships go. It is about looking on the bright side of all family relationships even if there is no communication.

This is about making our years ahead the best they can be so if we lighten our thoughts about family if we need to, we pave the way to age with grace and contentment.

Parents

At this stage of our lives our parents have either transitioned over or are quite elderly. Each one of us have our own personal view of parents even if you grew up in the same household with others because we each have a different way we think and feel about life so we experienced it in our own way.

If you got along well with your parents remember them with fondness and the memories you made together. Keep this love that you shared as a bright reminder that it is special and taught you how to feel this love for yourself and others. Share it with your own family in the exact same way so that it moves down to each generation and just keeps on going.

If you did not get along with one or both of your parents now is the time to revamp your focus as it is not helping you to be as healthy as you want to be both mentally and physically if you keep those emotions alive about issues from any time in your relationship with them.

Love yourself enough to do this. See yourself as the amazing person that you are and know that what happened in life regarding your parents does not characterize you.

Theirs was a generation of bringing forward what they in fact learned and they were not ones for thinking outside the box very much if at all.

If we have compassion for them, look at them through the wisdom that we have now it might seem that maybe they were unhappy and they just could not help the way they acted because of a dissatisfaction within themselves.

In their day not much was discussed about the state of things such as mental health, alcoholism or child abuse. So much was overlooked or accepted in our youth which made life possibly harder than it should have been but it was as hard for our parents too for there wasn't the openness of today for all parties to be able to get the help they needed.

Sometimes if we take a look at the events of our childhood at this time of our life we might possibly see where our parents may have not been where they would have liked to be, or they did have some problems that as children we just were not aware of.

A simple way to do this is take a situation that you have experienced in your childhood that has bothered you and think about it for a moment. When you have this thought clearly in your mind look at it now through your eyes at the age that you are instead of looking at it through those child-like eyes that you have always used. You may see things differently and notice things that as an adult you can understand a little better.

If we choose to have the attitude that our parents may have had issues beyond even their control, possibly had issues that we can now as adults understand a little better it brings out our compassion for others and allows us to move past this point for good.

It could be their behavior might possibly was a learned one from their childhood which was brought forward where they acted exactly as they were raised and chose not to be different.

If we practice looking at our parents with a kinder eye it eases the hurt and anger that some may feel about that time in their life.

When we speak of our parents we should be as upbeat as we can. Find the memories that are fun so that there are smiles when they are told and probably a few good laughs as well. By making a habit of finding the best thoughts and using those when we need to, we change the direction of the way that we remember our earlier life.

It doesn't change what was but it helps us to keep our thoughts in the best place we can when we reflect back to this time of our life.

The fact is that not all parents and children get along. For one reason or another they just don't gel if you will. It has to do with having totally different thought processes that just do not link with each other. Sometimes that is a difficult realization but it is a sound one because it means that there were personality conflicts that couldn't be overcome. Let's stop blaming anyone and start by letting go starting a new direction of thought making it the most positive we can.

It is time now for you to be the person you are today, to love yourself, to approve of yourself, and to remember that you have lived a full life and still have so much to do that who you are right now is the most important thing.

The only person's opinion of you that is important it yours. It does not matter about anything that anyone has said or will say about you, has done or will do to you, it is about knowing that how you feel about yourself is the most significant thing to you. Do not let anyone take that away from you.

It does not make you flawed if you could not make things work with one parent or the other or both for that matter; it just means you were different people that did not happen to think the same way.

If you want to remember one thing about your parents, remember their laughter. It was a high point in their life and the best part of them.

Positive thoughts on parents:

- I will look at my parents through adult eyes and life experience.
- I will think of positive experiences with my parents and keep that memory vivid.
- I will let go of hurts and anger directed at my parents so I can be happy.

Siblings

Siblings were as big part of our family dynamic as our parents since they were there throughout our growing years; they are part of those memories as well as a part of our lives as we matured.

If you have or had siblings, you know that they were a link to childhood like nothing else could be. They were there through all the highs and lows of growing up.

If your sibs and you are close and you do communicate with each other cherish this and strengthen it as much as you can. There is nothing like a sib to be able to talk to as they have known you the longest and understand you more because of all the experiences shared in childhood. As we age it makes it even more special because we are family and we are there for each other. Be thankful for them, appreciate them, and enjoy them.

I know that age, time and circumstances can alter relationships with siblings. As we age we do change our opinions and what we like and don't like, it is just a part of life.

There are also other circumstances that cause a rift between sibs some to do with family, some to do with spouses, and some to do with interaction that did not end well.

Again it may be that you just cannot get along, because individual thought processes are just so different that it makes it difficult if not impossible to have a connection or to keep one.

If for whatever reason you do not communicate with each other then I would ask this of you, let go of whatever you are harboring against them and let a peaceful feeling replace all that is negative in your thoughts of them.

Let go of the he said she said dialogue because it is of no use to anyone and makes the situation worsen with time.

There used to be party game years ago and it went like this:

Everyone would put their chairs in a circle. The hostess had a one to two sentence statement she would whisper in the first person's ear, this person whispered it to the next person and so on until it got to the last person in the circle. The last person then said out loud what was whispered in their ear and you guessed it, not even close to what was said in the beginning.

The point being that the more you repeat something especially if it is negative the larger it grows and the more out of context it becomes. It also makes you angrier or sadder or more hurt which in fact is making the negative in your life too prevalent. It is so detrimental to your well-being to stay in this negative way of thinking.

If there are issues with a sibling or siblings do not let it consume you. Understand that sometimes things happen that cause people to drift apart. It is like the parent thing, not everyone gels. But it is within your power to think of your siblings in the best possible light. This done on a daily basis lifts that dark cloud that follows anger and hatred.

Let's give ourselves a break here and just stop talking about who was wrong and who was right and just let it all go so that at least the energy that you were putting into it can be used for something much more productive in your life.

I am not advocating that you mend anything with your sib, if you want to that is strictly up to you, but what I am asking of you is that you let go of any animosity for your own sake and allow yourself the freedom of feeling at peace.

If you cannot be around each other then at least make the effort to think of them in the best possible light so that you feel good whenever a thought of them pops into your head.

Remember this is about you so as you work on how you can feel the best that you possibly can you must realize that by being angry or hurt any time that you think about your sibling you are not at your peak of well-being.

It is just time to let things go and to appreciate something about them that you admire or love and keep that thought in your mind so that the rest can just not be a factor anymore in your life.

No matter what has passed between you if you allow the peace of letting go of whatever it was surround you, then you bring into your life a time where you can think and feel in the most positive of ways and this is the goal for the years ahead isn't it?

Using your thoughts bring up some of the best memories you have of your sibs. I am sure you have several. It is our thoughts and feelings that bring about a change of attitude towards those we feel may have wronged us a one time or another. If we choose to think the best thoughts that we have in our memory bank of them then we choose to be on the path of being as positive as we can.

If you forgive and forget you are doing yourself the biggest favor you have ever known because your life is about choosing to feel good, about feeling love, and about having the years ahead be all that you want them to be. You will be getting rid of a burden on your heart that once gone will lighten your thoughts considerably.

If you want to remember something about your sibling try remembering a secret you shared as kids that was awesome.

Positive thoughts on siblings:

- I choose to remember my sibs with love.
- I have picked a time that was fun to remember them in.
- I have changed my negative thoughts about my sibs to the most positive I can think of.

Significant Others

Whether we have had one partner all of our lives or more than one the focus here is on well-being.

If you have a good relationship and you are content then this is something to commemorate. I am sure there have been ups and downs during your time together, you wouldn't be human if there wasn't, but this is something to appreciate and be thankful for. There should be many things to remember and feel good about over the years.

In our relationships together no matter the bumps along the way we should be recounting the best of times, the fun things that we did together and the accomplishments we have had. When we do this we reinforce the pleasure of our years together.

If you just found each other and your relationship is new, how wonderful to be able to share these years ahead with ease and peace.

Then there is the other side of the coin and that is to be unhappy and relive it frequently. There are many of us who have done this over the years and it is time to take a look at how it has affected us.

Some may be in a situation that is not as happy as they would like it to be. It seems that they have been waiting for years for someone to change to their liking and so far it just hasn't happened. They blame their unhappiness on the other person in the relationship and have a list of complaints a mile long they have accumulated over the years.

When you are living with someone and you are telling unhappy stories about life with them then you are making a negative impact on both of your lives. You cannot be happy if you are constantly talking about being unhappy.

Look for some way to change your focus so that you allow who *you* are to be as happy as possible. Your happiness is paramount to your well-being and having said that you must find the way to be happy.

Search yourself and think of ways that will help you to achieve a happy state of mind for your greater good. It may take some time on your part to figure it out but the effort will be worth it.

Since we have traveled to this point in life we know the things that we do enjoy, those that make us feel good. Keep your focus on doing these things and finding joy in your daily existence then you find that things in life change because you are looking at it in a better way.

You can ask yourself what can I change about my life that can help me to be the happiest I have ever been in this relationship. What would be different for me if I did change something?

We simply cannot expect another person to make us happy they can however enhance the happiness we feel about who we are. Depend on yourself to find the joy in life, the beauty and the happiness. You know what makes life this way for you so utilize it for your greater good.

The belief that someone has to change so that we can be happy is one way to be unhappy yourself. The only person that can change to your benefit is you others should not be expected to so that it fits your needs. You are the one who can make happy choices for yourself.

Truly we cannot expect another person to make our life what we want it to be. It is up to us to love ourselves and to be happy then it enhances our relationships because we are not expecting someone else to make our life the way we want it to be.

Remembering that each of us has our own thought process we must not expect anyone else to think the same way that we do. If we accept this it smooth's life's path quite a bit.

Another aspect in our lives is talking about partners that no longer are in our lives in a negative way. This can be an unending loop if we allow it to be.

If you are regaling stories of unhappy times regarding someone you were with at one time in your life then here is a place where changing your focus and letting go can actually almost create a miracle for you.

If you are bitter and angry you do not help yourself in any way, you certainly are not feeling good and when these thoughts consume you then they affect your wellbeing. Letting go here is imperative for you to feel the best that you can.

It is easy as we have discussed earlier to find the negative and be all over it talking about it and reliving it so that we are almost right there again in our mind. When we are constantly talking about times in our lives with another person and what was wrong with them, what they did wrong and where all of these instances added up to hurts and anger then we are harming ourselves with negativity.

When you decide to change that focus and not discuss anything about that time in your life unless it was positive you begin to heal all of those things that have still had you in turmoil even though they no longer exist.

There is nothing in your life that cannot be forgiven and forgotten if you choose to do so. It takes practice to stop yourself from regaling all that went on before that angered or hurt you but if you do stop you will find more interesting and fun things to talk about and guess what: your mood elevates to a place that is really good.

This part of your life, the part that *was,* no longer serves any purpose for you. When you bring it up you are bringing it back and what is the point when it makes you so unhappy.

If your significant other has transitioned over this is a whole different experience. It takes time to adjust and the grief is always present but it is great to celebrate their time here with you, to recall good times and fun adventures. Make the memory of them important and worthwhile for their time here was significant and beautiful.

Children

I have had a magnet on my refrigerator for years that says:

> *"You Can't Scare Me ~I Have Children."*

If anyone would have wanted to challenge us when we were young they could have very well said "Have children and see how that goes for you."

It was a great challenge wasn't it? There were joys and sorrows and every kind of emotion we have ever known tied up in our kids.

So many of our life lessons were learned from them in the process of getting them raised.

Our attitude towards our kids is very significant even though they are now adults themselves with kids of their own.

One of the most important things to think about is that their lives are light years ahead of where we were at their age.

Our attitude towards them needs to be of support and strength and understanding that things are most definitely different than they used to be.

Our children may have to reinvent themselves several times during their life. It is just the way things are now so we need to be the strength they can depend on as their lives change. Some of us have had to re-invent ourselves out of necessity which gives us firsthand knowledge of what that entails.

Why not encourage re-inventing, understanding that it is beneficial to do it and be on board with any thoughts that would assist them.

It is important for us to give them hope for their future, to be as positive as we possibly can about their lives and to set the example of thinking the best thoughts we can think about them and for them.

If they don't have hope then it is hard to be positive and there is always hope to be shared in one way or another. Try the very best that you can to be optimistic about all avenues of life so they can get a sense of well-being with you.

Be the example that things do work out when we look at the best side of life.

Be the example of consideration and compassion.

Be the example of thinking outside of the box and knowing that things can be done so many different ways and have the same result.

I know that some kids move slowly and some at warp speed but remember this is their life and they can't fit into a mold that you might think they should. If they are trying to fit into a mold of yours they most likely are not as happy as they could be making their own mold.

We all know from personal experience how fast things change in this day and age so if we embrace change then we encourage our children to see that it is nothing to fear.

They are unique as each human being is and they must find their way, a way that suits them, and they will do it so much better with your understanding that life is not one big do it the same way deal.

If you have had encouragement throughout your life then you know how it feels and should be passing it down to those you love the most. If you have not had it then start precedence now in your family so that it will be handed down for the generations that come after you.

This is not about doing everything for them; this is about building up the feelings of self worth and giving them the optimism of making life as they would like it to be. If they are confident about themselves build on that, if they are not start a foundation of helping them see the very best of who they are so that they can thrive in the parts of their lives they need to.

Our children even though they are adults still bring to our lives the wonderful emotion of love. Let's love them enough to boost how they feel about themselves and life. Let's help them to make a path through time that is one of positive thinking and seeing the good in the world, in others and in themselves.

If we point these things out to them then we are doing them a enormous service for then they are able to keep looking at life the greatest way possible.

Why would we not want them to be as happy as they can be, doing what is right for them. We cannot live through them or for them so the best thing we can do is to support them with our own positive thinking and the encouragement whenever they need it.

If we are ever changing the way that we look at life in general and are seeing only what is right about it we become the example for our children to start the same practice. When we point out what is good about them, what they think and how they are doing things then our relationships are at a very high point.

When we start talking in a positive way then they are more apt to listen to what we have to say. If we are encouraging and compassionate towards their thoughts and ideas then the feeling of unity between parent and child just grows stronger.

When we change with the times we not only grow as individuals we grow with our family and are linked in a way that helps keep all ties as strong as they can be.

When we make this shift to be in sync with everything our kids are living and doing then we can say that we are really in tune with this next generation.

Of course you will not give up your own identity; you will just be adding more zest to it. You will always be true to yourself with just more knowledge about what is going on around you.

As the senior generation let's be the example of seeing all view points of our children and accept that how someone else does it is just right for them so we then know a peacefulness that helps in aiding our own well-being.

It is better to be linked with our kids than at odds with them. No matter where they live whether it is the same town or miles and miles away there is always a way to be in touch, to keep positive conversations going so that they are encouraged to look for good things everywhere.

By understanding that they too have a thought process they work from that belongs solely to them, we can offer love, thoughts of our own, and encouragement to them while we let them be who they are and help them to live life to the fullest.

Positive thoughts on children:

- I will see life through their eyes.
- I will encourage new ideas.
- I will talk about life in the positive.
- I will share that I too had blips on my screen and overcame them.
- I will help them to have hope for their future and make it a constant to remind them life is good.

I understand that some of us have not had an easy time with our children even in adulthood, that there are circumstances that sometimes are impossible to even be a part of what is going on in their lives. I also understand that some of us have lost our children and are coping with the loss.

I would say this to you if you are in fact one of these people:

Celebrate them and think of them with love and kindness. Even though there is grief and sadness combine that with the joy of their existence, think of them as the beautiful spirit they once were and celebrate the fact they made a difference in this world at one time. Bring up your happiest moments and no matter what age they were when difficulties began or death came about remember them with appreciation and love for they were once and still are shining stars.

Grandchildren

I have another magnet on my refrigerator that says:

"If I Had Known Grandchildren Were So Much Fun I Would Have Had Then First."

To say that grandchildren are special is not even close to describing what we feel for them. They are for most of us the sun, moon and stars.

Those that have them know what I mean; there is no feeling like it as they bring such joy and love into our life that is stronger and more beautiful than any other feeling we have known.

Since our grandchildren are so important to us have you ever considered how our attitude about almost everything affects them?

Do you have any idea what an influence you are on them and how you act and react makes such a difference because they look up to you which makes you a role-model?

Here is your time to shine. This is where you can be an example that can change the attitude of a whole generation.

You can and you will if you choose to be a prime example of kindness, compassion, patience, and love.

Talk about re-inventing yourself, it would make you the grandparent who shows their grandchildren how to make the world a better place.

Who knew?

You could choose to point out everything that is positive about them, build their love of self and the confidence to go forward to be all that they can be.

This is the time to let go of all pessimism or criticism, this is the time to see the beautiful spirit that they are, looking forward with great hope to the future, and you can be the one who encourages them to be all that they are and more.

It is a time of supporting their ideas, to be linked with them even more so that you are a part of their ever evolving thoughts about life.

Our grandchildren's generation is so technologically ahead of what we have ever seen that they are going to know a world we have not even imagined. When your grandchildren know more about technology right now than you do it speaks volumes of where their generation is going.

Why not help them see life as an adventure, one that is positive, fulfilling and happy? You can be the best example by staying upbeat and helping them to recognize everything positive that is around them and recognizes everything positive in what they are doing.

My dad used to say that his youth was the best time of life in this country, which was the twenties and thirties he so fondly remembered. I know that each of us feel that we came from the best time, the best generation, that it was the most fun, but the fact is; that time is so far behind the point the world is at today that we must get into the swing of where our grandkids are living and thinking.

I remember dad talking about racing Model T's in his youth and I would think to myself how old is that when kids are driving Corvette's? Just think about how much farther ahead life is now from when those Corvette's were new.

Since we are living in this moment, in the now it is time to get with the grandkids mind set.

What if we stopped finding fault with the kids today and realize that there are more good kids out there than not?

What if we set the example for our grandchildren to learn patience, kindness compassion, to feel hope and joy? Aren't these the traits that we would love the world to have more of?

I would challenge you at this time to find hope if you don't have it now for the world, the people in it and especially your grandkids. If we have lost our hope that the world still is a wonderful place to be then we can't encourage any generation.

Remember when we were kids and nuclear war was the topic every day? Think about it, we are still here, the cold war has been over for such a long time and all of the worry and fear that people went through came to nothing.

I am sure it is because more people believed in peace and wanted that far more for the world.

We must have hope; we must have the mindset that there is good around us and happening all over. If we can show our grandkids all that is right with our world then we start a thought pattern not only in our generation as we point out these things but in their generation and our children's as well so that hope becomes the focus, hope becomes the way we think and hope then leads to things happening for the better.

If we live right now in this time and space and show our grandchildren how to appreciate all of the good things going on around them, to treat others as we would like to be treated, and to show compassion for those that need it we will make huge steps forward in the way life progresses for us and them.

Our attitude is their guideline as they watch how we act and react to situations and issues. How we relate the state of everything around us is paramount to how they see life and in what element they see it.

If we show patience in situations where it is needed then they learn patience. If we show kindness to others then they too will act kind, if we show compassion for issues around us then they will understand that we do feel concern for our fellow man.

But if we are constantly criticizing the world, the people in it, if we are rude and uncaring, if we are unkind when we communicate with others, then we are showing them a way of life that does not benefit them in any way but the negative.

If we are afraid they learn fear, if we worry then they too will be anxious. Children are like sponges they soak up everything that is said to them or that they listen to so please think about your dialogue making sure it does not affect them in the negative.

We want the best for them there is no question about that, so the part of the best for them can be the example we set for their well-being.

Seeing our grandchildren and the unconditional love and joy that they feel about us, about their parents and about their lives in general is a good thing to encourage because it is really a foundation in which to build a life that is fulfilling and happy.

Of course they will learn more as they age but by focusing on all of the good things in their lives while they are young is the basis of how to make those thoughts grow so that they know life's beauty and happiness along the way.

Isn't it wonderful to be the one to show enthusiasm and encouragement to those that are just starting their journey?

Isn't it great to take the responsibility of showing them that there are more good things than bad, that they are important part of the world, that they do and will make a difference, and that by being positive they will feel the best they possibly can?

This is an important undertaking as you are cheering on a small person to make their journey fun, showing them with your attitude that life is best when seen through the eyes of someone that recognizes the good everywhere.

I had two grandmothers that were great examples of strength and love. They were both independent and strong. They both were very family oriented and that has stayed with me till this day. There were many things that I learned from their actions.

My maternal grandmother was full of sayings about life. If we would fall down when we were kids and be crying she would always say "You'll forget about it when you get married." I make my kids laugh when I use one and I always start out with "Jane used to say."

If you had grandparents that you looked up to and made an impact on your life remember what it felt like to have that and enhance those examples by using your attitude towards the positive as the guide for your grandkids.

If you didn't have a grandparent experience that was fondly remembered then be the one you would have liked to have had. Be the one who takes the time and effort to help your grandchildren be the best they can be, as you do this you will make memories for them that they will carry forward and use in their own lives.

Just imagine the impact we could make on the world if we did in fact help our grandchildren's generation find all the good things about life and focus on those.

We also teach them about safety and smart thinking that goes without saying. We do live in a different world today, but having said that there should be no fear instilled so that it impairs their daily life.

By showing them through example how to treat our fellow man with kindness, with patience and with compassion they too will know the good feelings that this brings to a person which then brings more of the same as you do feel good and you do benefit from being this way.

They won't know this unless you show them through example. So the next time you need patience look for it somewhere inside and show them what it is like to use it. Use kind words when you speak to people, smile as much as you can. See you are feeling better already aren't you?

Let's give up the speeches about today's younger generation and how terrible the world is going to be because they are not what they should be. Didn't you hate hearing that when we were growing up? Guess what: we didn't end the world and neither will they.

How much more negative can you be if you tell your grandchildren how bad their generation is?

We had our time and it was great but now it is their time and we need to get on board with helping them figure it out.

If you want them to have a good lives then help them to find it.

That is what it is all about isn't it. You want them to feel good, to have fun and to enjoy their youth. While you are the example of all of this you are also making it easy for them to see just how to treat others and to make a difference in our world for the better.

I would ask you now how do you think your attitude is and how do you think it affects your grandchildren? For their greater good how could you have a different one so that they could blossom and grow?

Positive thoughts on grandkids:

- I will listen when they talk to me about what interest them.
- I will encourage them to do well in school.
- I will point out all of their strengths.
- I will show them how to have fun,
- I will be a sounding board if they need one.
- I will let them know that I too experienced some of what they have and it all turned out okay.
- I will not try to make them think like I did when I was their age; that ship has sailed.

Friendships

We have several treasures in our lives, our children and grandchildren being among them and I must add friendships to the list.

These are monumental relationships and they are very important at this phase of our lives.

The friendships we have cultivated over the years from childhood on are so wonderful because these are the people we chose to have in our lives. That makes them the most special of people because they lift our spirits, know so much about us, and are a constant for us in every important occasion of our lives.

The fact that they know so much about us and still love us is incredibly special. They have been and still are solid and reliable and they are exceptional people we can talk to, they listen, and they do not judge (well maybe just a little bit but they get over it.). They lend a sympathetic ear and help us just by being there or giving their opinion if we need one.

So I would say this about this stage of our lives and friendships; strengthen them, the ones that mean the most to you especially. Take the time to stay in contact more often so that you are uplifted every time you have a conversation.

If our attitude about friendship is one that is caring and we look at them as special then we connect with those that we have things in common with, that make us feel good when we are with them, and help us stay in our positive frame of mind because it is in fact so much fun to visit with them.

What a tailor made feel good way to live, people who bring joy into your life with their company and conversation.

Get together as often as you can and enjoy each other. Laugh and have fun, find positive things to talk about so that you do feel very good when you are finished visiting. By making a habit of being the most upbeat you can be you find that it brings to your life the feeling of well-being and the knowledge that you are in fact a person who thrives on the best things in life.

We are at the point in life where having people to have fun with should be a priority. What better way than to have the wonderful friendships we have refined throughout our lifetime and take advantage of these great people and the joy they bring into our lives.

Our conversations are important to the way that we feel when we are together and when we leave each other. Let's make it a habit, when we are together with our friends, to talk about the good things that are going on in our lives, our children's lives and our grandchildren's lives. Let's make it a point to be as upbeat as we can and enjoy the laughter and happiness that goes along with being with people who make you feel good.

Cherish each and every one of them and appreciate the communication whether it is being in the same town, e-mailing, texting or phone calls. Thank heavens for modern technology and how it affords us the ability to keep in touch in so many ways.

Make the effort; you will be so glad that you did. We all have those friends that have transitioned over and of course we miss them but the memories we made with them, the special place they have in our hearts are a testament to keeping friendship alive and well until we can't.

Positive thoughts on friendships:

- I love to be with friends and share laughter and fun.
- I will contact friends more often that help me to feel the best that I can feel.
- I will make the effort get together with those friends that mean the most to me.

CHAPTER 12

Health and Well-Being

"It is not how old you are, it's how you are old." — *Jules Renard*

A ge: one of the stages of life

How we think and feel about aging and its affect on us is so important. It is the basis of how we see ourselves now, how we feel now, and how we go forward into the next phase of our life.

There is a very important approach about aging and that is you are as old as you think you are. Age is just a number; it shows us where we are on the scale of life from where we started but it does not dictate anything more than how we think about it.

When we were discussing children and grandchildren it was done with a more youthful approach to the subject because we are not the typical seniors that have preceded us, we are the seniors now that do have a much younger attitude and by having this attitude we are less elderly and much more hip to the day and age.

This is our time to excel, our generation has the choices to look and feel the best any senior generation has before us.

There should no longer be any hard and fast rules about aging. There should only be what rules we set for ourselves, ones that we choose to fit with our lifestyle. The one hard and fast rule about aging is our frame of mind, our focus and how they tie into our well-being.

Let's rid ourselves of the stereotypes that have been made before us. Let's show the world that aging only has to do with the way we think about it and how we use those thoughts for the greatest well-being we have ever known.

If we take pride in who we are at this moment, how we look, and practice feeling the best that we can, we will set the standard for aging to a new level.

If we start the day by taking pleasure in our appearance, looking around us and appreciating all that is good, and focus on our health being the best it can be then how could we not know well-being?

We all want to feel the very best that we can both physically and mentally. It is very important to have positive thoughts about both state of mind and physical health so that it becomes a habit to have the best frame of mind possible.

Our Physical Health

Health: a condition of optimal well-being.

If we are the generation that is to change aging for the better there are a some things that we can look at and see if in fact by letting go of negative thoughts about any health issues we may have or have had and beginning to look at our health in the best way that we can, we can make a difference in how we feel physically and mentally.

If you could visualize your health exactly how you would like it to be what would it look and feel like? Picture yourself for a moment and see yourself just as you want to be health wise. How do you feel when you are looking at yourself in that mode?

I am sure that you see yourself in the utmost health and well being and it wasn't that hard to imagine when you put your mind to it. So why not make a statement to yourself that this is in fact what you want your health to be and you intend to do the best possible thinking about your wellbeing that you can.

The first thing you should do when you wake up in the morning is a happy dance because you did in fact wake up. After the happy dance there are choices you can make about what to observe that feels good about your body.

The choice to see yourself in good health daily is up to you. If you start the day expecting to feel good that is a very positive beginning.

Here are some what if's to consider:

- ❖ What if we noticed everything on our body that works perfectly and focused on those?
- ❖ What if we expected good health every day?
- ❖ What if we focused on our body working the exact way it should in every part?
- ❖ What if when we focus we expect our body to keep up with the good thoughts we have about our health?

How we talk about our health is also very important because we are telling a story that is literal and our focus is right where the story is.

- ❖ What if we chose to let go of all the negative stories when we are discussing our health?
- ❖ What if instead we talked about the positive things that have come from the medical procedures we have undergone, or the illnesses we have recovered from?
- ❖ What if we make the discussions about how much better we feel, how much more mobile we are, and how much we appreciate our health and well-being?
- ❖ What if we let go of every preconceived notion about what our health is suppose to be as we age and put in place our own notions of what we want it to be?

It truly is about choice and how you might choose to change talking about health and health related issues to be the most upbeat they can be.

Our attitude could be one of acknowledgement that we have the medical techniques which can take care of so many health issues today that make our lives much easier.

Some of us are bionic with all the replacement parts that we have but the fact is we are pain free because of them.

The truth is we should be elated to be aging in this era of fast track technology.

We have medical expertise that cares for our hearts now without much fuss, there are replacement parts galore, and there are so many surgeries that are same day which is remarkable.

We must look at our good fortune to be in this place and time where things are so easily medically taken care of for us.

We are smart enough to know when something is not right and seek medical assistance when we need it. Use your amazing intelligence about your health and if in fact something is off call your doctor and talk about it. You know your body and how it feels. Be smart and use the wisdom you have gathered over the years to stay in the best of health. Take care of yourself, take the meds prescribed for you, and think only of being the healthiest you can be.

When you think about your health see your whole body functioning as it should, the numbers they use in the medical profession being exactly what they should be, and do not doubt that thinking in the positive is key to your well-being.

When we use our thoughts in this way our body responds to those thoughts. We are actually guiding how we feel by thinking only the best things about our bodies. Let your body know you trust it to be well and use the most positive thoughts about your health and well-being.

Remember this; fear is a negative faith. Do not let fear be a part of your thoughts of health. Trust that we have so many ways to be well the most important is how we think about being in perfect health.

Another important factor is to keep busy doing things that interest you, that you enjoy making your days filled with moments of satisfaction. Each one of us has their own things they like doing many have several. Keep yourself doing what brings you the most contentment so that you can feel really good about your days.

By using a strong focus on good health and keeping busy so that our minds are sharp then we start a great pattern for feeling great. If we expect the best from our bodies, if we expect our bodies to function at the highest level possible, then how can our bodies not respond at a very high level going along with the thoughts we give it.

It is as simple as thinking the best or the worst. I know it can be a habit to share stories of ill health detailing what was done and how it was done and where it was done but when relating these stories whether it was you or someone else you are surrounding yourself with the negativity about health that you do not need. Here is yet another instance of letting go of situations that are not serving you in the way that you want your life to be.

We all know that we want the best for the years to come so thinking about perfect health is a bonus isn't it? We can do this if we make up our mind that this is the course we want to set our mind on.

Let's be the healthiest senior generation ever, and let's do it by using our thoughts to reinforce the best well-being in each of us. Let's only talk about what feels good concerning our health and start a trend of who can feel the best by doing just that.

Here are some thoughts that may help start your day in the most positive way:

- I start each morning thinking of perfect health and how great I feel.
- I take care of my appearance so that I feel energized.
- I do things that interest me daily so I can keep myself healthy both mentally and physically.
- I take my medication faithfully so that my body works the best that it can.
- Each evening when I retire I think of all the good things that happened to me during the day.
- I see my physical health as always improving so that my body tunes into this thought process.

CHAPTER 13

The World and how it affects our Attitude

"The world as we have created it is a process of our thinking. It cannot be changed without changing our thinking." – Albert Einstein

If we are to be the generation that changes aging then our view of the world should be that of hope, faith and the beauty that does exist out there.

It has become easy to see and talk about the worst case scenario all of the time. For some reason we as humans just love finding what is wrong more than we try to find what is right. It is strictly in how you decide to see the world.

There are a few things you can choose to do that change your outlook every day so that you can make your own world peaceful and calm. Just think about these suggestions and see if you can realize the validity of them.

Okay news junkies here it is: *turn it off.* Oh I know that several of you are thinking no way is that going to happen but if we take a look at what we are doing to our well-being when we are embroiled in all that is being reported we might take another look at how it affects our daily life.

There are news programs, newspaper, and the internet where we can hear the absolute worst possible things going on in our town, our country and the world. These sensational stories are magnified and repeated so many times that after a while who could possible feel good about life in general when tuned into all of this negativity.

We hear stories about people of the world, celebrities, politicians, and so many others. The first thing we do is make a judgment about it. Start talking about their misfortune or what we think about it. The truth is we only know what it told to us we have no idea of the circumstances or what the whole picture is just what is reported.

It is all about that he said she said thing again When you only get one or two parts of the whole story how can we possibly judge by that?

Another thing is why do we care about others people's lives especially those in turmoil?

What if we just refused to bring all of this chaos into our life?

What if we opened up the way we think and allow the concept that not everything is bad, the world is a beautiful place to be, and the way we think about it is very important in the way we feel? You know; the ray of sunshine instead of a dark cloud.

What if there is as much good going on in the world than there is bad? Could it be possible that there is more good going on out there than bad but it just isn't sensational enough to talk about?

What if there are more people with goodness and kindness in this world than there are not. We really need to make a point of believing this so we start to recognize those people in our daily lives and the area that surrounds us.

What if we had compassion for those in trouble instead of criticism?

Wouldn't it be great to have a news channel that only broadcasts the good news in the world? I know it would because I belong to a group on Face Book that only posts fun and happy things this is the one rule to belong and I will guarantee you that I get so many posts from all over the world all day long that it is fun just to sit and watch them come through. Some are posts of the good that others are doing all over the globe so I know there are people who care about others, who are compassionate and kind.

There are people on our planet that are making a difference in a good way so if you want to see the goodness in the world don't tune into the news on television or the news on the internet, instead search for good things to read about or see.

The internet is a great source of inspirational stories of humanity. The world has so many people doing things for the greater good of the planet and mankind. There are thousands of stories of good works you only have to search for them to find them as they are not reported nearly as often as they should be.

There are people with disabilities who make the news who will make you feel wonderful by the things that they have accomplished even though they have limitations. Search a few of these out, you will be amazed at how you will feel this right into your soul. Their happiness and joy is very contagious and serves as reminder that we too can reach for the best feelings possible if we put our mind to it.

We don't have the limitations that these inspirational people have and yet we tend to be more cynical and jaded. This is really time for an attitude adjustment when we are not as grateful as we should be and contented with life as those less fortunate physically and mentally as we are.

Be inspired by those who are doing good things in our world, by those who have embraced life even though they have challenges, and by those who's kindness and compassion are making such a difference around the globe.

It is our choice to look for the good in our world whether it is in our backyard or on the planet. If we choose to let go of negativity of any kind regarding the world and the people in it we are one step further in making our lives feel as good as they can.

It of course is a choice but I would ask you why not?

If we are the generation that is improving the way that we think let's do it with the intention of looking inside first for the love, the happiness the beauty and the joy that we each have. Then let's make it a point to see that in the rest of mankind, the place that we live and the world.

What if we choose to just start the day without any outside interference from the news whether it is television, internet or newspapers?

What if we chose to start our day with the thoughts of those we love, the thoughts that make us the happiest, and the thoughts of all that surrounds us that makes our life beautiful?

Whatever these things are for you are just right because we all are going to have different ones. The most important thing is that how they make you feel and how you can be much more lighthearted about life when you do this.

If we take on the problems of the world each morning we don't have anything left for our own well-being.

Isn't it at this stage of our lives time to put our own well-being the top priority so that we can enjoy the coming years to the fullest and become more and more peaceful and calm.

If we are right in the middle of all things that are reported to us in a negative way and we are feeling it, then discussing it, and possibly arguing about it how can we feel good?

If we just let go of needing to be right or in control and we let go of anything that brings us such anger or unhappiness because of something we heard or read about the world's condition or the people in it, then we start on a path that brings even more peace that you can imagine.

Let's not let outside influences become so entrenched in our daily lives that we lose sight of our well-being and the ability to feel great joy and peace.

If it is possible for you to let go of the news and anything related to it you will see a large change in your attitude about life in general.

Positive thoughts on how you might start your day with instead of the news:

• Today I will aim to feel as happy as I can by thinking of things that do make me contented.
• Today I will use my thoughts to feel joy from deep inside my heart.
• Today I will look at the beauty all around me in every place I can find it.
• Today I choose to live in the moment.
• Today I choose to anticipate only good things happening in my life.

In place of the news turn on some music and let that help you to start your day in a way that brings a better frame of mind to you. Each of us has our own style of music and by listening to it we can then begin to form the thoughts that help us to be more positive. Besides music just makes us feel good.

Let's not rely on outside sources to start our day, instead let's choose to start with our own style, our own enjoyment so that we can feel the command of well-being just happen for us.

Imagine if you would that each one of us took the responsibility for starting each day with the most positive thoughts about ourselves, our community and the world.

Imagine if you would each one of us made the effort to see the good in everyone.

Imagine if you would we each make our surroundings and those that surround us the happiest they can be.

I know you can feel the power in this, the fact that each of us will be making our own space, our own part of the world the best that it can be.

CHAPTER 14

It is all about Mind-Set

*"We can complain that the rosebushes have thorns, or rejoice because
the thorn bushes have roses." – Abraham Lincoln*

Mind-set – a person's attitude or set of opinions about something.

Our mind-set is the most important thing about us and if we use it to our greatest advantage then we will have the best part of our lives ahead.

It is strictly up to you of course on how you look at your life, where you attitude is as far as your well-being, but I ask would you this question:

Why would you not want to feel the best that you can feel, use your thoughts in the best way possible and focus on all that good things in your life?

Some people will think it is too hard to go from the negative to the positive and I always smile at that because it really is *your* mind-set and *you have control over the thoughts you think* so instead of looking at life in the worst way simply turn it around and look at it in the best way.

If you want to feel good then your mind-set would be on thinking about things that make you happy, people you enjoy and places that have been a positive influence for you.

When we choose to see life as an adventure and then choose to look around us for all the good things that are happening, have happened and anticipate even more happening then we open our minds to pinpointing all of those things and holding on to them instead of anything else.

It does take practice but it is well worth it for the feelings of happiness that we get when we do this outweigh the effort of changing the way we think.

What will your mind-set be for the rest of the journey ahead?

You know how you want to feel both physically and mentally, how much contentment and peace you want in your daily life, which makes it possible to have the greatest experience aging can bring.

There isn't one of us that do not want the best years ahead for ourselves so I would challenge you to delve into where you can change your attitude for the better in your life and then make the effort to do so.

Remember this: you are you and no one else. You are not your grandparents, your parents or your siblings. You have refined yourself over all of these years and now you can be who you want to be just by using your focus on all areas of your life for your greater good.

By making the effort to change how we are focusing and using our mind-set to looking with hope and joy at who we are and how we can make life the easiest it can be by enjoying all of it in the moment then aging should be a breeze.

"Your age does not determine your well-being, your attitude towards it does." – Sue Asti Cortesi

Positive thoughts on mind-set:

- My mind-set is very important to my well-being so I choose for it to be the most positive it can be.
- I choose to change my mind-set so that I can feel the best I have ever felt and keep feeling this way every day.
- I will make a habit of starting the day with the very best mind-set I can.
- I am a unique person who knows how I want to feel so I use my focus to the best of my ability.

CHAPTER 15

Are You Up to the Challenge

This entire self-help guide has been about thinking outside the box and allowing a whole new idea about how to age and how to make the rest of our journey the very best part of our life.

It is about intentionally choosing to practice being the most positive you can be when you are focusing on anything in your life.

So I would say this to all of you in this baby-boomer generation. Let's be the ones who do change how we are looking at life and make it the greatest change any generation has ever seen.

Let's make the difference in the world that is so noticeable it cannot be ignored.

Here are some challenges to give ourselves every day:

- To become the examples of hope, of seeing the world in the best light, of showing each other kindness and caring.
- To let go of anything that is holding us back in a negative way to a life of joy and happiness.
- To keep our thoughts about self so good that we start each day realizing what a great person we truly are.
- To focus on what is right in your life and let everything else go.
- To support your adult children and the challenges that they face in a constantly changing world. To be non-judgmental, to see they may need to reinvent themselves or recreate what they are doing. Be a fountain of knowledge but with the idea that it is their time and times change constantly.
- This is an important one; to be the example of hope, joy and love for your grandchildren, to guide them to love themselves, to be who they are and to shine in the world. You can do this and if you do you are helping to change the world in ways you won't believe.
- To think of your health as being the best it has ever been, so that your positive thinking is helping your body to respond to having perfect health.
- To notice daily things of beauty around you along with things that helps you to feel joy.
- To laugh every day and have fun.

The biggest challenge here is for each of us to make our own space and who we are happy. That would be the catalyst if you will to making a huge difference in the world.

Imagine if you would if each of us just took the responsibility for their own happiness, didn't worry about anyone else, what they thought or what was going on outside of our own space. Just paying attention to ourselves and making everything in our own personal world the best it could be.

Think about how much positive energy would generate from that everywhere.

There is great power in this and I am sure you can feel it just by reading about it.

I have encouraged you to help your children and grandchildren to be the best they can be but I would like to ask the same thing of you.

This is your time to shine and it is as easy as thinking the best thoughts you can think and being happy right where you are in the here and now.

So here is the greatest challenge: Be happy, focus on the most positive things around you and make your well-being your top priority.

If each person took responsibility for their own happiness and well-being what a different world we could make.

Positive thoughts on mind-set:

- I will make the effort to keep my mind-set in the now concentrating on what is right about my life.
- I will be thankful for the fact that I am able to choose what I think about so that thoughts can be just what I want them to be.
- I choose to look at each area of my life where my mind-set makes a difference and change it to the most positive it can be.

CHAPTER 16

Making a Statement

They say a picture is worth a thousand words so why not use your thought process to help you daily to achieve the mind-set that benefits you the most.

Here are a few visualizations that can help you picture different parts of your life in positive ways.

It is important when you are using these to be relaxed and in a quiet space for the time it takes to do them. Once you have found your comfortable spot take a few deep breaths and feel yourself loosen up then use any one of the vision statements.

Starting the Day

As I begin my day I will embrace a positive mind-set. I will make a point of noticing everything that is good around me at the start of the day. I will count my blessing and as I do more and more keep coming to mind which makes me feel good.

I will look forward to the day with hope and the belief that all is well.

I will make the effort to talk kindly to everyone and smile often. In all of the conversations I have today laughter will be a part of them; I am going to make the effort to laugh as often as possible.

And as I start my day I will be so thankful for all of my life experience, all the happiness that has come into my life over the years and for the fact that I am at this point and still smiling.

My intention starting this beautiful day is to feel good, to embrace the positive, and to keep my focus on my well-being.

End of the Day

As I am getting ready for a restful night's sleep I am going to allow myself to relax by just breathing steadily and using my focus to appreciate the day that I have had.

While I am thinking about my day I am going to let go of anything that was not positive for me. I know that it is my choice to hold on to or let go and for my greater good I am going to clear my mind of anything that does not help me to feel good. So as I let go, just breathing steadily and relaxing I feel those thoughts drift away and I clear my mind completely I am now ready to think of the most pleasant and positive things about my day.

I choose to think about things that helped me to feel good, people who I enjoyed, and situations that were positive for me. The more I think of these things the more that remember. I remember the laughter and the thoughtfulness of others.

By choosing to use my focus for this intention I now am relaxed and have very good feelings about my day and how it went.

I do realize that more positive things happened for me today than anything else and it helps me to consciously recognize them and confirm that positive things happen to me all of the time.

And as my breathing is steady and I feel completely relaxed I will be able to drift off to sleep easily and enjoy a restful night.

Love of Self

As I take several relaxing breaths I picture myself and the beautiful spirit who is me.

I am happy with my personality and the ability to laugh and enjoy life. I love who I am. I have made a difference in the world just by being me.

I see all of my strengths and how they have helped me so far in life and I know that I do have the strength to make my way forward with a great sense of well-being. I appreciate my life as it is right now and look forward to enjoying years ahead with a very positive outlook.

I will only see the good things about myself and focus on them. As I do this I find that my feelings towards who I am is the best they have ever been.

My focus about myself is that of caring and love for I deserve it.

I will appreciate everything I do well and the more I recognize those things the better they look.

I am one of a kind and it takes me and only me to fill my space here on the planet to the best of my ability.

I know that my beauty comes from the inside and I appreciate that I can use it when I smile at others, speak an encouraging or kind word to someone.

I feel myself become stronger and stronger the more positive I feel about who I am and everything I have done.

Life is good and I intend to think of it that way constantly.

Letting Go

As I take several relaxing breaths and as I feel my breathing become very steady I am ready to let go of something that is not helping my well-being.

This issue that needs to be gone from my heart and mind is ready to leave and I am more than ready to let it go.

I sit here and steady my breathing.......just letting it go in and out and relaxing my mind as I get ready to clear my thoughts.

As I picture what I want to let go of I feel it becoming lighter and lighter on my thoughts. I am clearing it completely out of my mind set and as I do this I can see it erasing itself completely from my thoughts. I can actually feel how much weight is lifted from me and I know now that this is the only way for me to feel the way I want to feel all of the time.

There is something else I would rather think about.....this thought is a happy one and I want to replace now the one that I let go of with this good one.

I will now make the effort to not bring it back.....if it should pop up at some point I will choose to change it with the happy one I have chosen to take it's place.

I now feel free of all that was and I am ready now to be in a better place mentally for my greater good. I am ready to focus now on everything that makes me feel good as often as I can.

Attitude

As I take several relaxing breaths I feel myself searching for the attitude that will help me to be the most positive I can be.

I am seeing in my life all that is good, I am noticing things that as I look around please me. I choose to think of the happiness in my life and focus on feeling good.

I want to be in the frame of mind that helps me to be the healthiest and happiest I can be. By choosing to do this my attitude is helping me to do just that.

My attitude is the most important thing to my well-being that I have so I am choosing to make it the most positive it has ever been before.

I understand now that what I am thinking about and how I am thinking about it makes all the difference in how I feel and how I act. I want to make my attitude that of someone others enjoy being around, one that I can feel good about myself, and one that has me in the best frame of mind I can have.

Focus

As I take several relaxing breaths I find it is easy to focus in this type of setting where it is quiet and I am relaxed.

By choosing what I wish to focus on it makes me realize that I have had this option all along and never took full advantage at using it for my greater good.

I choose now to focus on something that helps me to be in a positive frame of mind. My focus will be something that helps me to feel good.

By using a positive focus I am reinforcing that I do want to be the most upbeat I can be during the day. This helps me to feel good and to make the difference in my life that I intend to.

Every time I change my focus during the day I find that I am looking only for the upbeat and positive. I find that a focus point is all about what feels good to me.

It is easy now to focus on things around me that make me feel good and it has become a habit to notice these things continually.

The beauty in life and those that are around me give me so much to focus on. I find that I discover more everyday.

Every time I use this statement to focus on something that helps me stay positive it can be a different one each time or the same one it does not matter because my focus is about me and only me and it helps me to center myself in a way that is for my greater good.

Aging

As I take several relaxing breaths I begin to see aging as an adventure. I have come this far with so much experience and I now want this time of my life to be the finest.

I will make the effort now to see aging in a different light, letting go of anything negative I may have thought and embracing everything positive I can think of.

I will appreciate all the technology that is out there for me when I need it. I will be thankful that I am able to use it and take advantage of all the positive things it brings to my life.

I will appreciate that the medical world is at its best and I am in the most knowledgeable time regarding medicine that has ever been.

As I see myself aging I know that all is well when I think the most positive things I can about life, health and well-being. I will make the effort every day to be the most optimistic about my age and my life.

I will see aging as a journey and I will keep myself busy doing things that I enjoy so that as I age I do it with grace and pride.

I will embrace aging with a smile because I know it is my attitude that will make all the difference for me.

My intention is to be as healthy both mentally and physically and I also intend to be mobile and enjoying all facets of my life at this point.

I have had a tremendous journey so far and now I want to concentrate on aging as being one of the brightest parts of it.

I will take it upon myself to use my thoughts in the best possible light in all areas of my life and use my attitude for my greater good.

Being Calm

As I am sitting quietly I take several deep breaths allowing my body to relax. As my breathing becomes even and as I breathe in and out a complete sense of well-being moves over me so that I feel very calm and relaxed.

I notice that my breathing is very calming to me and as my breaths become a little deeper my mind clears completely and I am just paying attention to the way I breath and the feeling of calm that becomes stronger and stronger for me.

Being calm is like ripples on a lake, once it starts it just keeps moving and moving from the inside of me to all parts of my body. The feeling of calm just moves slowly through me and I find that it is very easy to bring forward as I just sit all allow it to move though me.

I feel all of my muscles just relaxing as my body and mind are completely calm.

I will sit here now for a while and just let myself unwind, enjoying the fact that I am calm and relaxed. This feeling is for my greater good and I will use it to be well.

Feeling Happy

As I take several breaths and I sit quietly I think of a happy time in my life and focus on those feelings that remembering brings to me.

I love the feelings that come with this memory so I just concentrate on all of the nuances of that time and what it meant to me.

It brings me great pleasure to remember this time, it also reminds me that happiness is a feeling which is a part of who I am.

Once I start thinking of happy times in life it seems that one after the other appear in my thoughts so I realize just how often I felt this way.

I understand that happiness is at the core of who I am and I have felt happiness over my lifetime, so much so that it makes me feel good just to understand that.

I love to feel happy and my focus is to stay in this state of mind as often as I can so that I have a wonderful sense of well-being.

I will make the effort to stay in a happy frame of mind each day.

Peace

As I take several breaths and I sit quietly I imagine a very peaceful setting that is familiar to me. This is a favorite place for me so it is easy to think about and visualize. I just sit here for a few minutes in this spot and let myself be.

I realize as I sit here that my breathing is even and slow, it relaxes me even further as I visualize and breath and have a completely peaceful feeling surround me.

As I slow my mind in this place that is quiet and calms me, the feeling that I have as I sit here is amazing.

This is such a peaceful place to be there is nothing here that isn't easy and free. Using these thoughts I find peace within myself and a feeling of contentment that helps every part of my body.

My body responds to all of these wonderful feelings and I find that I can do this so easily when I just let go and allow peace to enter my mind.

I will use this peaceful feeling all of the time to help me with my day to day routine. When I do I know that I am taking care of myself and I am in charge of my well-being.

I want to keep a peaceful attitude about life so I will use this peaceful feeling that I have right now knowing that it does exist for me I just have to sit for a minute and focus on it and it is there for me to experience anytime I want it.

The Best Health Ever

As I take several breaths and I sit quietly I am so thankful for my body and all it has done for me over the years.

My intention every day it to focus on everything that is right about my health and to appreciate all of the things I am able to do as I focus on feeling the best I can feel.

I know my attitude must be the most positive it has ever been regarding my health so I will make the effort to think and speak in the most healthy and optimistic way.

I refuse to think anything negative about my well-being because I understand that my body responds to my thoughts and feelings. I will try my hardest to keep my conversations and thoughts the most encouraging they have ever been regarding my health.

I will take care of myself in ways I know will benefit me and I will be constant about seeing myself in the most positive light possible.

I am ready to start each day feeling great and noticing that when I do this it makes a big impact on my life.

My focus is the best health possible so I tune into what feels the best about my body and appreciate all the things I can do.

I realize when I do this that each day my body responds favorably to the use of positive thoughts. The better I feel mentally and physically the better life gets for me.

Quotes in this book came from: www.goodreads.com/quotes
All definitions came from: www.merriam-webster.com

Printed in the United States
By Bookmasters